A New Look at an Old Earth

What the Creation Institutes are **not** Telling You about Genesis

Don Stoner

D0382442

SCHROEDER
PUBLISHING

13119 Downey Ave., Paramount, CA 90723

A New Look at an Old Earth,
What the Creation Institutes Are Not Telling You About
Genesis,
By Don Stoner

Cover design: Chris Michika
Earth photo courtesy of NASA

Schroeder Publishing Company
13119 Downey Ave., Paramount, CA 90723
(310) 923-2311

ISBN 1-881446-00-X
First printing, this edition: July 1992
Printed in the U.S.A.

Table of Contents

Acknowledgements

There are too many people – scientists and theologians, old earthers and young earthers – who have helped with this project to list them all here; and I fear I may forget someone if I try; still, I would like to make one mention: It is the intent that this book be comprehensible to a tired mother of five at 11:00 P.M. at the end of a hard day. I would like to thank my wife Debbie for providing the feedback to make this goal possible.

Foreword
By Dr. Hugh Ross

James, the brother of Jesus, in addressing the council at Jerusalem declared, "It is my judgement, therefore, that we should not make it difficult for the Gentiles who are turning to God (Acts 15:19)." The apostle Paul in his letter to the Romans said, "Make up your mind not to put any stumbling block or obstacle in your brother's way (Romans 14:13)." Don Stoner challenges us in the following pages to remove a great impediment to the furtherance of the gospel of Jesus Christ.

Instead of focusing on the now overwhelming evidence for the God of the Bible and on the complete accuracy of His Word, many within Christendom would have us discount this potent new evidence, all for the sake of clinging to the rather peripheral (to the Gospel) dogma of a recently-created universe.

This digression has effectively inoculated a large segment of secular society against taking seriously the call to faith in Christ. It also has divided the Christian community into hostile camps that focus more energy on attacking each other than on reaching nonbelievers. Worse yet, the nation's courts have come to perceive age as the central issue for the creation/evolution debate. Thus, a pretext has been provided – the lack of credibility for a thousands-of-years-old universe – for removing the Bible and the concept of creation from public education.

As Mr. Stoner emphasizes, science is man's attempt to interpret the facts of nature, while theology is man's attempt to interpret the words of the Bible. God created the universe and also is responsible for the words of the Bible. Since He is incapable of lying or deceit, there can be no contradiction between the words of the Bible and the facts of nature. Any conflict between science and theology must be attributable to human misinterpretation. Such conflicts should be welcomed, not feared or battled, for they point the way to further research and study that could resolve the apparent discrepancies.

Historically such resolutions have not only born the fruit of bringing warring parties to peace and fellowship but also provided new tools for winning souls for Christ. It is in this spirit that this book is written, and it is in this spirit that I hope this book will be read.

Chapter 1:
Judging Ourselves First

"Why do you look at the speck of sawdust in your brother's eye and pay no attention to the plank in your own eye? How can you say to your brother, 'Let me take the speck out of your eye,' when all the time there is a plank in your own eye? You hypocrite, first take the plank out of your own eye, and then you will see clearly to remove the speck from your brother's eye."

—Matthew 7:3-5.

It would be nice to be able to show scientists who are atheists the error of their ways and to lead them to Christ. It would also be nice to be able to remove some untrue "scientific" teachings from our public schools' curriculum. But before we correct others, we must apply Jesus' admonition (quoted above) and remove errors from our own position.

Because our position is founded upon God's word the Bible, we might assume we have made no errors. Unfortunately, it is easier to make mistakes about facts than we normally suppose — even about Biblical facts.

Consider the passage in Isaiah describing peace between all animals during the millennium. This makes such a beautiful picture that it is often the subject of paintings and statues. We have all heard preachers describe this scene to us on numerous occasions; but do we really know what the Bible says about even this familiar scene? Does Isaiah mention some predator which lies down with a lamb?

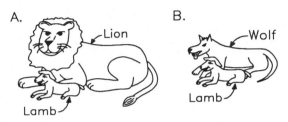

Isaiah 11:6

Most of us "remember" that the lion and lamb will lie down next to each other; but this is *not* what the Bible actually says! What Isaiah 11:6 says is:

"The **wolf** also shall dwell with the **lamb**, and the leopard shall **lie down** with the kid; and the calf and the young **lion** and the fatling together; and a little child shall lead them."

−K.J.V. Emphasis mine. See also Isaiah 65:25.

In fact, as a few minutes with a Bible and an exhaustive concordance will prove, the Bible *never* describes this scene exactly as most of us "remember" it.

For another example, most of us "remember" that Jesus stumbled and fell while He was carrying His cross; but again, the Bible doesn't actually tell us this. We know that Jesus carried His own cross (John 19:17); we also know that Simon was forced to carry it (Matt. 27:32, Mark 15:21, Luke 23:26); but we can only speculate as to why Simon might have taken over. The Bible simply doesn't tell us this.

It is easy to confuse what we have merely heard with what the Bible actually says. If we hear something repeated often enough, we are likely to accept it as Biblical truth. We hear things from people we trust and tell those things to others who trust us. We hardly ever stop to apply the scriptural admonition:

"Test everything. Hold on to the good."

– 1 Thessalonians 5:21.

Still, this may not sound too important. It doesn't really matter whether or not Jesus actually stumbled while carrying His cross, or how many types of animals will lie down in which combinations during the millennium. These questions are not really central to our faith; but are we any more careful when the questions *are* important?

Consider an example which relates to death as a consequence of sin. In the second chapter of Genesis, God gave one commandment which, in Adam's day, was all the law that existed:

"Of every tree of the garden thou mayest freely eat: But of the tree of the knowledge of good and evil, thou shalt not eat of it: for in the day that thou eatest thereof thou shalt surely die."

– Genesis 2:16, 17, K.J.V.

This single commandment was all Adam needed to understand and obey. As Christians, we still look back to this verse to sharpen our own understanding of what Jesus' death means for us; but do we understand what this verse means? Did Adam really die in the day he sinned? The Bible tells us that he lived for many years after he ate the forbidden fruit (Genesis 5:3, 4).

Most of us have heard from people we trust that Adam died **spiritually** rather than **physically** in the day he sinned. Many of us have even explained this to other people who trusted us; but how many of us have critically examined this interpretation to see if it is the truth? Because it is not a literal interpretation, we have good reason to be skeptical. To test this, the accepted method of comparing scripture with scripture must be applied. There are several places in the Bible where death is referred to as a consequence of Adam's sin.

For example, consider how Jesus died to atone for Adam's sin. The Bible tells us His death was **physical**. We see in the gospels that there was no way that the crucifixion could be avoided (Matthew 26:39, 42, Luke 24:20, 26). If **physical** death could have been avoided, it would have been. In fact, it would appear from the resurrection that Jesus did not die **spiritually** at all.

Romans 5:14 presents another place in scripture where we can test the nature of Adam's curse:

> "Nevertheless, death reigned from the time of Adam to the time of Moses, even over those who did not sin by breaking a command, as did Adam, ..."

Here Paul is using the obvious fact that all men between Adam and Moses died **physically**, to prove his claim (from back in verse 12) that sin and human death entered through just one man; but notice also that Paul considers these **physical** deaths to be so firmly an effect of sin that their existence proves the presence of sin − even where no specific law has been broken. If this were not true, Paul's argument would be worthless; if Adam's sin only brought **spiritual** death, the **physical** deaths of all those men would prove nothing about sin's presence or absence.

Scripture teaches that Adam's sin brought **physical** death upon mankind and that Jesus had to die **physically** to atone for it. Whatever **spiritual** aspects might be involved, and regardless of their importance, the related references confirm the **physical** aspects. Where death is spoken of as being the result of sin, the counsel of other scripture teaches that **physical** death should be assumed irrespective of what decisions are made about including or excluding **spiritual** death. God even confirmed this **physical** aspect within the curse which He pronounced upon the ground after Adam's fall, "... for dust you are and to dust you will return." (Genesis 3:19).

In Romans, Paul uses "death" in a **spiritual** or **figurative** sense:

> "Once I was alive apart from law; but when the commandment came, sin sprang to life and I died."

> −Romans 7:9.

Here Paul describes a kind of "death" which results when knowledge of the law gives sin an opening (see also Romans 7:11). This is different from Adam's death which resulted from his **breaking** of a law which he had already heard. Although related, Paul's <u>spiritual</u> or <u>figurative</u> death is not quite the same as the death which results from Adam's original sin. We die <u>physically</u> because Adam sinned – whether or not we have heard the law; we do not die in the sense Paul describes until we have heard the commandment.

The correct way to interpret Genesis 2:17 is that Adam was to die a literal <u>physical</u> death in the day he ate the fruit. It is an accepted rule of interpretation that the <u>literal</u> meaning of a word in scripture should be preferred over a <u>spiritual</u>, <u>figurative</u> or <u>symbolic</u> one whenever possible – especially when closely related scripture confirms the <u>literal</u> meaning.

There is still the problem that Adam did not die <u>physically</u> until long after he sinned. God's command places the execution of judgement within the same day as the act of disobedience. Might we be misunderstanding the word "day?"

The book of Genesis, like most of the Old Testament, was originally written in Hebrew. The word "day" was translated from the Hebrew word "yom" which, not surprisingly, means "day."[1] In fact, the *present-day* usage of our English word "day" is almost an exact equivalent of what "yom" meant back when Genesis was written. It even carries the same alternate meanings. For example, both can mean: twenty-four hours; the twelve hours in which the sun is shining;[2] a moment of glory;[3] or even a time period of indefinite length.[4] When a person speaks of "the present day," (for example, in the third sentence of this paragraph) he is using the word "day" in the "indefinite period" sense. Notice that this usage is <u>literal</u>, not <u>figurative</u>, <u>symbolic</u> or <u>spiritual</u>. The "present day" is not a poetic comparison to a

---

[1] <u>Gesenius' Hebrew-Chaldee Lexicon to the Old Testament</u>, C. 1979, Baker Book House Co., Grand Rapids, Michigan, p. 341, (entry #3117). According to Gesenius, the primary signification is the **heat** of the day but the word is used in a wide variety of ways.

[2] For example, "forty days and forty nights," Genesis 7:4.

[3] English example, "every dog has his day." Hebrew example, Hosea 7:5.

[4] Genesis 2:4 is normally assumed to refer to the whole creation period.

twenty-four-hour day; it is a **literal** time period of indefinite length. Likewise, the Bible sometimes uses the Hebrew "yom" in contexts referring to periods of greater length than twenty-four hours. For example, it is believed that "the *day* of the Lord," (Isaiah 13:6, 9), will last more than twenty-four hours.[5]

The related verses indicate that Adam died a **literal physical** death in the "day" he sinned; it follows that the "day" in question must have been a time period of indefinite length. This very simple and quite **literal** understanding of the word "day" cleanly eliminates any problems.[6]

It is easy to be wrong – even about important verses; but at least no real harm has been done. Perhaps we were too trusting when teachers we respect explained to us that Adam merely died spiritually. Maybe those of us who have spread this error should be more careful. Still, this is not very serious. It is not like gossip – where people might actually be hurt by the careless spreading of tales.

This brings us to the reason for this book. It is almost universally taught in evangelical Christian circles today that the earth is very young – about ten thousand years old or even less. We hear this repeatedly from teachers we respect and trust. We ourselves may have spread this teaching to those who trust us. But is this teaching the truth or an error?

How old does the Bible say the earth is? The Genesis account says it was created in six "days." But what does the word "day" really mean? How long were the "days" of Genesis? This is the same question which we encountered regarding Genesis 2:17. Once again, a Biblical "day" is not necessarily twenty-four hours long.

It is difficult to simply read the first chapter of Genesis and come away with any but the six-consecutive-twenty-four-hour meaning; but how much of this is because of the actual wording of Genesis and how much is because of what we have simply heard? Do the actual words of Genesis *really* make literal sense

---

[5]Zechariah 14:7 is another example.

[6]The N.I.V. Bible translates "yom" as "when" in Genesis 2:17 to make this intended meaning clearer: "... you must not eat from the tree of the knowledge of good and evil, for **when** you eat of it you will surely die."

to us? "And there was evening, and there was morning – the first day." (Genesis 1:5). What could a literal "morning" possibly mean before the sun was "made?" (Genesis 1:16). Furthermore, the "plain English" which a modern reader encounters is not quite the same as the original Hebrew. Genesis might be harder to understand than is normally assumed.

The first chapter of Genesis is an ancient work; for this reason, it might be difficult to understand. Consider this verse from The Faerie Queen,[7] by Edmund Spenser, first published in the year 1590 AD:

> A gentle Knight was pricking on the plaine, Ycladd in mightie armes and silver shielde, Wherein old dints of deepe woundes did remaine, The cruell markes of many' a bloody fielde; Yet armes till that time did he never wield. His angry steede did chide his foming bitt, As much disdayning to the curbe to yield: Full jolly knight he seemed, and faire did sitt, As one·for knightly giusts and fierce encounters fitt.
>
> – Book 1, Canto 1, Verse 1.

To a modern reader, the term "curbe" (curb in modern spelling) seems to mean something like a command to "halt." But this makes the rest of that line confusing. The term actually refers to part of the horse's bit. In this example, the *correct* literal reading is *not* the plainest one! "Yielding to the curb" can even mean "being run off the road" in today's "plain English." This was written a mere 400 years ago and in an archaic form of *our own* language; yet it is still difficult to understand.

By comparison, the first chapter of Genesis was written in Hebrew, and thousands of years ago by even the most conservative estimates. There is evidence that the Hebrew may be a translation from a yet older account.[8] The original was probably written even before the sun and moon were given

---

[7]The Faerie Queen, Edmund Spenser, J.M. Dent and Sons Ltd., London, and E.P. Dutton and Co. Inc., N.Y., 1910 edition, p. 19.

[8]Ancient Records and the Structure of Genesis, P.J. Wiseman, C. 1985, Thomas Nelson Publishers, Nashville, p. 20. This is an excellent book – highly recommended.

proper names.[9] Notice that they are simply referred to as "great lights." It is difficult even to imagine an account of this antiquity.

Because we have difficulty understanding Spenser, who is relatively recent, we have no guarantee that a plain reading of Genesis 1 will make any sense at all to us. It is likely that we will have to be very careful if we hope to understand the creation account correctly.

As will be shown, there is an old-earth understanding of Genesis which is consistent with every detail in God's word – only we will have to keep our eyes open to see it. The young-earth point of view is *not* the only possible understanding of Genesis 1; in fact, as will also be shown, the young-earth position is incompatible with the scientific evidence which God's creation provides. .

Scientists can easily determine the age of God's creation. It speaks of its own age in many different ways. As will be shown in following chapters, there is no escaping the antiquity of the earth. It is billions of years old. The scientific evidence is very clear. The Bible itself even implies that a study of God's creation will reveal that the earth is *very* old:

> "Since the creation of the world God's invisible qualities – his **eternal** power and divine nature – have been **clearly seen**, being understood from what has been made, so that men are without excuse."

> – Romans 1:20, Emphasis mine.

God is *eternal* and powerful. His creation says so. Scientists have *clearly seen* the agelessness and power of God's creation from their own personal observations and measurements. They know who God must be.

What happens when we Christians tell scientists that the Biblical text *cannot* be harmonized with an earth which is billions of years old? Scientists conclude that the God of the Bible is *not* the God of creation. This is because they have clearly seen God's creation and *we* have told them the Biblical one is different! We have told them the Bible limits the age of

---

[9]Ibid p. 88.

the universe to about ten thousand years; and they believe it must. They *trust us* to understand the Bible and they take our word for what it says and means. Because they trust us, they will not bother to check the Scriptures for themselves. They simply conclude the Biblical account is untrue.

Of course Romans 1:20 also says that scientists who do not recognize their Creator are "without excuse." Could it be that we are giving them one? If they trust us to give them an excuse to die in their sins, why won't they trust us for the whole truth? The problem is that we have failed to remove the "plank" from our own eye first. As Jesus told us in Matthew 7:3-5 (quoted at the beginning of this chapter), we must fix our own eye before we can see clearly enough to fix our brother's eye. We must have the right understanding of what Genesis really means if we are to see clearly enough to correct the scientists. Any false assumptions we make will certainly damage our attempts; if we are wrong, the scientists will know it and will not listen to us. As always, judgment should begin with the house of God (1 Peter 4:17).

Unfortunately, it is difficult for those of us who are not scientifically educated to tell the difference between scientific truth and error. An unsophisticated error will often be more alluring than the plain old ordinary truth. Because of this, we are unconsciously drawn to the wrong arguments. We enjoy mocking university graduates. Juicy claims about how some Ph.D. has misread the facts are circulated from Christian to Christian just like so much gossip. We hear these stories from those we trust and pass them on to those who trust us. Unfortunately, we never bother to find out if any of these stories are true.

We have been mocking educated men and, what is worse, we have done it from a position of blind ignorance. We have made fun of the fossil hunters; but how many of us have even held an authentic fossil in our own hands? We have called the men who dated those fossils fools; but how many of us would know how to date a fossil ourselves? Do we care enough about knowledge to study the fossils ourselves? We must ask ourselves if *we* aren't really the fools; does Solomon's description fit us?

"Wisdom calls aloud in the street, she raises her voice in the public squares; at the head of the noisy streets she cries out, in the gateways of the city she makes her speech: 'How long will you simple ones love your simple ways? How long will mockers delight in mockery and fools hate knowledge? ... '"

– Proverbs 1:20-22

Even those of us who would never intentionally lie will thoughtlessly pass on almost anything we hear just so long as it appears to glorify God. We are much too gullible. We should always confirm information before we spread it to others. We should not pass on tales about the men who date the fossils unless we are willing to make sure those stories are true. And how can we make sure? Sorting truth from error requires careful testing. This cannot be accomplished by simply selecting those stories which please our ears. The truth is not always pleasant to hear!

In keeping with the spirit of this chapter, one last comment is in order. During the writing of this book, the Lord has been teaching me[10] how easily serious mistakes can be made. This has taught me to be more forgiving toward mistakes made by others. Making mistakes is an unavoidable consequence of being human; and I am as human as anyone is. Although this book has been checked over by many theologians and scientists, there are undoubtedly many remaining errors. Because this book deals, in part, with errors which have been made by our brothers in Christ, its errors are likely to be quite awful! My desire is to remain as much at peace with my brothers as is possible. Although this book is a necessary correction, it can't be emphasized enough that the young-earth creationists and I are on the same side where it counts. Although they are in error concerning a lesser issue, we are both working for the same ultimate goal. Perhaps the age of the universe should never have been made into an issue in the first place; unfortunately, it has been made into a serious one which must now be resolved. I apologize in advance for any hurt which I may inadvertently cause; it is my goal to restore unity, not to fuel division.

---

[10]Here I needed to step forward; in the rest of the book I will hide behind the awful title "this author."

Chapter 2:
Science, Theology and Truth

"Test everything. Hold on to the good"

– 1 Thessalonians 5:21.

One goal of this book is to prepare Christians to lead scientists to Christ. In order to accomplish this, we must first remove the "plank" from our own eye; this means the young-earth position must be refuted (Chapters 3, 4 and 5). Another goal is to present Biblical creationism in the context of an old universe (Chapter 6). Yet another goal is to better acquaint Christians with their Creator by bringing them to a better understanding of His creation. These are ambitious undertakings to say the least.

Because readers are not expected to be scientifically educated, scientific information will be presented and explained as it becomes necessary for understanding. This book will gradually become more technical as it proceeds; those who endure to the end should be properly prepared to present their faith to non-Christian scientists.

Before a knight can battle dragons, he must first learn to hold his sword. Likewise, we must start at the beginning. First, the meanings of a few basic terms will be reviewed. Even with so modest a first step, readers are liable to be in for a surprise or two.

Consider the two terms "scientist" and "Christian." These two are sometimes thought of as opposites – which they most certainly are *not*. A person who is a scientist is not necessarily a non-Christian and vice versa. The world is comprised of:

> 1) Christians who are also scientists,
> 2) Christians who are not scientists,
> 3) Scientists who are not Christians,
>   and amazingly,
> 4) People who are neither scientists nor Christians.

This carries an important consequence: just because a teaching is scientific does not make it non-Christian! Scientists are *not always wrong*. Just because a scientist (even one who happens to be an atheist) believes that water freezes at 32 degrees Fahrenheit does not mean that Christians must believe otherwise. Likewise, just because a scientist (even one who happens to be an atheist) believes the earth is old does *not* mean that Christians must believe it is young. It is not necessary to disagree about everything.

Next, consider four more basic terms: 1) the Bible, 2) the universe, 3) theology and 4) science. These terms relate as follows:

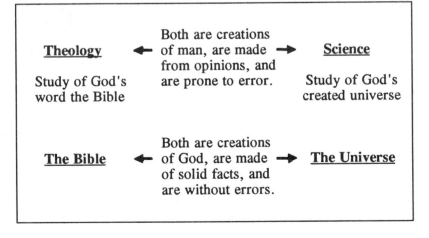

Theology	Both are creations of man, are made from opinions, and are prone to error.	**Science**
Study of God's word the Bible		Study of God's created universe
The Bible	Both are creations of God, are made of solid facts, and are without errors.	**The Universe**

Of course this diagram is not totally complete; among other things, it ignores the spiritual realm and the fact that the Bible itself makes statements about the physical universe; but it will serve to demonstrate a few things.

For example, a scientist must have faith in the actual facts concerning the universe in exactly the same sense that a theologian is expected to have faith in God's word, the Bible. The universe supplies evidence to support scientific theories; but what assurance does a scientist have that *its* evidence is valid – or that the universe will tell him the same story tomorrow? It is not difficult to imagine a universe with *invalid* evidence; most of us dream in one every night. A scientist's belief that the universe will tell him the truth must, in the final analysis, be taken on faith.

Likewise, a theologian should always regard his Biblical theories with the same sense of skepticism with which a scientist is expected to regard scientific theories; he can be wrong about the Bible just like a scientist can be wrong about the universe. Even his cherished rules of Biblical interpretation are fallible creations of men; they must *never* be confused with God's word itself. If it were not possible to interpret scripture incorrectly, there would be no false doctrines among us; there would not even be different denominations!

When a theologian tries to compare the Bible with science, what is he really doing? The two terms which he selects, "science" and "the Bible," provide a clue; the comparison is not a symmetrical one. The theologian studies the Bible directly but he views the universe indirectly through science. He, correctly, regards the Bible as being inerrant and science as comprising opinions; at any conflict, he will side with the Bible. A theologian who is not scientifically educated may even favor his fallible rules of interpretation over the universe's solid physical evidence.

Now when a scientist makes a similar comparison, he does so from a different vantage point. He studies the universe directly but tends to get his information about the Bible indirectly through theology. He, correctly, regards the universe as being inerrant and theology as comprising mere opinions. Naturally he will resolve all conflicts in favor of the universe.

Adding further complication to this picture, a "pure" scientist should not begin with any presuppositions as to whether or not the Bible contains valid data; of course scientists who are either Christian or atheistic will unavoidably have such presuppositions. A scientist who is an atheist will always place his fallible theories above the Bible's inerrant text.

Considering this difference in approach, it is not too surprising that both theologians and scientists sometimes consider each other to be a little foolish; they both think their own position is founded upon solid evidence while the other's is based upon mere human opinions. Problems even arise between those scientists who acknowledge that the Bible is God's word and those theologians who believe that God's universe speaks the truth.

What both the theologian and the scientist often fail to realize is that they are usually comparing theological theories about the Bible with scientific theories about the universe. When it comes to our general understanding of things, facts simply do not speak for themselves; they must be interpreted in the light of theory. The resulting disagreements are not too surprising as both sides will often be making errors.

If the Bible could be compared directly with the physical universe (the bare scientific facts), there should never be any disagreements. Unfortunately, this is difficult to do; it is impossible to be sure that either is being understood correctly. In order to have a useful understanding of either the Bible or the universe, theories must be formed by which the various facts are understood and interpreted − for example: the doctrine of the Trinity (to explain apparent contradictions in the nature of God) or the theory of relativity (to explain apparent contradictions in the nature of time and space); and whenever theories are devised, mistakes are possible.

Theories, Facts and Errors

The way in which theories are constructed will be reviewed here. There are no scientific "scriptures" (other than the universe itself) to guide scientists; so they have worked out their own system which they call the scientific method. It is similar to the methods of interpretation which theologians have worked out to help them understand the Holy Scriptures. There is nothing sacred about the scientific method nor about the methods theologians use. Both are fallible creations of men. Neither is recorded in God's Bible nor in His physical universe. They are merely well-thought-out tools which are useful in seeking after truth.

In principle, the task of a scientist is to study the world around him in order to figure out the rules which govern its events. There is an old joke about a scientist who is studying a frog. He has trained this frog to jump on command. When he says, "Frog jump!" the frog jumps. He then cuts off the frog's legs and repeats the command. The frog does not jump. The scientist then concludes that the legless frog did not hear the command – that it must, therefore, hear with its legs.

This joke illustrates a difficulty with scientific inquiry. There is usually more than one possible explanation for the same observable facts. Sorting the right explanation from the wrong ones can require many well-designed experiments. Typically, the scientific method involves many cycles of looking at the evidence, formulating rules to describe the evidence, making predictions based on those rules, and then looking at the evidence again to see if the predictions were correct.[1] The more often this cycle is repeated, the more confident a scientist can be that he understands what he is studying.

No matter how many experiments are performed, scientists can never be absolutely sure about anything. In fact, our scientist might remove the legs from a dozen frogs and still not know the truth. Even if he had been removing ears instead of legs, he could not be certain that he was not disabling the frog's ability to

---

[1]This author will present some predictions of his own in Appendix 1 for those who are interested in following his theories as more information becomes available.

jump in some unexpected manner. Although scientists are confident that a frog *does* hear with its ears, this is more of a well-tested belief than a strictly proven fact.

Generalizations can never be proven true but they can easily be proven false. Even one conflicting fact will refute them. If our scientist were to train a frog to croak on command instead of having it jump, he could easily prove that a frog did *not* hear with its legs.[2]

In the real world, scientists are able to invent general rules which will explain all they see and which will predict the results of every experiment they perform for hundreds of years. Then, along comes an exception. The Michelson and Morley experiment, which will be examined in Chapter 4, is such an exception. This is how science works; a generalization is never known to be true with absolute certainty; but even one conflicting fact will refute it.

If scientists are limited like this, it seems strange that they can perform useful work. Yet they *certainly can* accomplish great things. They discover cures for diseases, put men on the moon, invent terrible weapons and do a great deal more. Although they are not always right, their system *does* seem to work for them most of the time.

Scientists are successful because they are able to sort their generalizations into different categories of certainty. Three categories which they use are "hypothesis," "theory," and "law."[3] These terms will be explained here – and also the term "fact" – but it must be kept in mind that there are no firm rules about how they are to be used. Different scientists tend to use them differently.

When a scientist climbs into a spacecraft and is launched into space, he puts his life on the line. Space launches are dangerous, but amazingly, most of them work as planned. Where his life is concerned, a scientist will trust only those generalizations in which he has the most confidence. When a scientist's reputation is all that is riding, he might be willing to "lighten up" a little.

---

[2]Or at least he could prove that a frog did not hear *exclusively* with its legs.

[3]The level of confidence can also be expressed in mathematical terms. For example, 99.7% sure.

When he is privately discussing new ideas with other scientists, his wildest speculations are acceptable.

The lowest speculative level of certainty is labeled "hypothesis." An hypothesis is merely a first guess. A scientist who has never been outdoors in his entire life might hypothesize that all leaves are red. This, although false, could nevertheless be a perfectly good hypothesis – at least until an actual leaf was examined. If the examined leaf happened to be green, then the hypothesis would be refuted; it would no longer be valid.

The scientist might then hypothesize that all leaves are green. Now, when another green leaf is examined, the hypothesis will be supported rather than refuted. Of course a second green leaf does not prove the hypothesis to be a fact; it only tends to confirm it.

The next step up the chain of certainty is called "theory." The term "theory" is actually used to mean two slightly different things. One meaning of "theory" describes an hypothesis which has stood up under some experimental verification. Assume that our scientist has made his generalization (all leaves are green), has made predictions based on the rule (all of the leaves in a particular garden will therefore be green) and has verified that his predictions were correct (those leaves, when examined, did turn out to be green). At this point, he might say that it is his "theory" that all leaves are green. Although he still doesn't know for sure, he is more certain after checking all the leaves in a garden than he was after he had examined just one leaf.

Even after making this additional progress, if one single red leaf were ever found, it would still refute the generalization that "all leaves are green." Our scientist would no longer have a valid theory or even a valid hypothesis. The generalization would merely be an error. Of course, the scientist could start over again with a different hypothesis. If he had found the red leaf during the month of August, for example, he might hypothesize that all leaves are green during the springtime.

At this point it is natural to ask how much experimental verification is required to promote an hypothesis to theory. There is really no single answer to this question. Experiments are all different and so the decision is somewhat arbitrary. Different fields of science require different levels of experimental verification before the promotion is recognized; and this promotion is never formal. Physics typically requires the most verification – psychology perhaps the least.[4] The level is set purely as a practical matter depending on the difficulty of performing experiments and how precisely the results of the experiment can be interpreted. A physicist can be more certain in one afternoon about how a rock falls than a psychologist can be in a lifetime about how a human brain works. Psychologists are, as a practical rule, permitted to promote their generalizations with much less confirmation; and consequently, their theories are either more cautiously worded or are more frequently incorrect.

A second meaning of the term "theory" describes *any* idea structure which can be used to explain some of the world's facts. This idea structure usually provides a reason why; for example, the reason all leaves ought to be green is that chlorophyll must be present for photosynthesis, and chlorophyll is green. Even a first hypothesis can also be a "theory" in this second sense. Further, even when the generalization attains the confidence level of scientific "law" (described below), it will still be a "theory" in this sense. The term "theoretical basis" is sometimes used to describe the reason why. For example, the theoretical basis for organic evolution is that mutations are random and that the fittest resulting individuals tend to be the ones which survive and reproduce.[5]

The final step in confidence is from "theory" to scientific "law." A law is a theory which has proved to be correct every single time it was tested by anyone, anywhere, for a very long period of time.[6] Physicists, for example, seldom promote a

---

[4]In fact, not everything which is lumped under the general heading of psychology is even science at all! Psychoanalysis, for example, does not follow the rules which would qualify it as one. See The Feynman Lectures on Physics, Richard P. Feynman, C. 1963, Addison-Wesley Publishing Co., Reading, Massachusetts, Vol. 1, p. 3-8.

[5]This author believes that God was responsible for the design of every one of His creatures – that random processes played no significant part in this. He also believes that minor "evolutionary" change occurs within each of the kinds which God created. This is responsible for minor adjustments. Here random mutations and survival fitness are the primary guiding factors.

[6]As we have mentioned, there is no rigid rule governing how these terms are to be used. For example, the geological principle of superposition is sometimes referred to as a "law" even though there are known exceptions. (Although not strictly true, it is still useful as a general rule.) The Cambridge Encyclopedia of

theory to the status of "law" without first testing it for many decades. Before this step is taken, all rival theories should be eliminated; a generalization is only regarded as a law when it is the only known way to explain the world's data (or at least the simplest of the known ways).

If our scientist had never been able to find a single leaf which was not green, and if he and many other scientists had been searching for one for many years, it might be proper to say that it was a scientific law that all leaves are green. Still, this would not make it a "fact" in the normal sense of the word. There would always be the chance that someone might discover a red leaf one day.

The finding of a single red leaf would refute a law that all leaves are green just as it would a theory or hypothesis. Our scientist's statement that, "All leaves are green," would, as before, simply be an error. He would be forced to start completely over again with a new hypothesis.

There is no recognized category of certainty for generalizations which is higher than scientific "law." The status of "fact" is not scientifically attainable for any inferred generalization. The term "fact" is restricted to the observable data.[7] For example, it could be a "fact" that one particular leaf was green at one time.

Because there are a lot of scientists working busily away at sorting out each other's ideas, a great deal of progress has been made. Before a scientist's theories are even published, other experts in related fields are permitted to poke holes in them. Scientists take great delight in proving each other wrong; consequently, they keep each other in line. For this reason, it is very unlikely that you will ever read in a scientific journal that a frog hears with its legs; but this is still no guarantee that

---

Earth Sciences, Ed. David G. Smith Ph.D., C. 1981, Crown Publishers Inc. / Cambridge University Press, N.Y., p. 387.

[7]But again these terms are sometimes used in different ways. One author uses the term "fact" to describe the once believed inferred generalization of Telegony. Because Telegony was an error, he also uses the term "false fact." Hen's Teeth and Horse's Toes, Stephen Jay Gould, C. 1983, W.W. Norton & Co., N.Y., pp. 379-380.

everything you read will be the truth. Scientists are human and humans sometimes make mistakes.

Seeking Truth

Although theologians sometimes fail to admit it, they are really in the same boat as the scientists. They have God's written word; but they have no written directions telling them how to interpret it. In the final analysis, this means they encounter the same problems the scientists do. Theologians are human too.

The young-earth teaching is the result of theologians forming dogmatic theories after examining the Biblical part of the evidence and paying insufficient attention to God's creation. This is almost as bad as trying to understand God's plan of salvation using only the Old Testament. The information in the Old Testament is much less specific; mistakes will invariably be made. Furthermore, once the wrong understanding has been reached, no amount of explaining away the additional facts of salvation found in the New Testament will ever make that first misunderstanding true. Only a discarding of the first error and the forming of a new theory using the combined data from both testaments will bring a person to the truth.

The same principle applies to a mistake about the age of God's creation. Once the mistake has been made, no amount of explaining away the rest of the evidence will ever turn that error into the truth. It is necessary to start completely over again and study both God's Bible and His universe together as a single unit. It would be foolish not to pay close attention to any evidence which God's universe might directly supply concerning its own creation – nearly as foolish as ignoring God's written account.

Both the Bible and the universe must be interpreted in a manner which does not contradict *any* of the actual facts contained in the combined whole. When a conflict is found between our understanding of the Bible and our understanding of the universe, we *must not* look for errors in either the Bible or the universe; we must look for errors in *our understanding*. It is the intent of this book never to contradict a word in scripture nor an observable fact of God's creation.

This method of seeking truth is not strictly scientific or theological. When it proves necessary, we will freely discard the sacred **methods** and **theories** of either side in favor of the other side's **facts**. *Be warned!* We humans are unaccustomed to this technique. It will undoubtedly irritate individuals from both professions. If you, dear reader, happen to be either a scientist or a theologian, then prepare yourself to be subjected to indignity after indignity in this book. It will remind scientists of the Inquisition where their carefully designed theories were judged and condemned under the Holy Writ. Theologians may feel they stand before a calloused heathen who condemns honored church teachings for no better reason than a few dusty fossils.

This book will fly in the face of the cherished beliefs of nearly everyone. Readers will often feel attacked. This is natural whenever comfortable old ideas are challenged. Although this book confronts old **theories**, it will never contradict the **facts** found in either God's scriptures or His creation.

Even with both science and scripture as our guides, there is still room for us to make mistakes. History teaches that it is possible to be wrong even when science and scripture both seem to agree with a person's beliefs. Before Galileo, most scientists[8] believed that the earth was the stationary center of the solar system and that the sun orbited around it. Those who studied the scriptures found them to be in agreement. In this case, both the scientists and the theologians were wrong! When Galileo began teaching the Copernican system – that the earth orbited the sun – he was attacked from both sides. Galileo was a Catholic and believed that his teaching was in agreement with the word of God. Still, he was regarded as being both a heretic and a bad scientist. Here is what the Inquisition had to say about his teaching:

---

[8]It would be more accurate to call these men "scholars" than "scientists" because in their day science was not separated from other studies (such as philosophy) as it is in ours. This author has used the word "scientists" here because it conveys the correct flavor of his intended meaning better, to his intended readers, than the more correct "scholars" would have.

"The proposition that the Sun is in the centre of the world and does not move from its place is absurd and false philosophically and formally heretical, because it is expressly contrary to the Holy Scriptures."

— From Galileo's sentence by the Inquisition.[9]

In case any readers still haven't got the word, the earth does orbit the sun — not the other way around. The idea that the sun travels around a stationary earth is not only very old fashioned, it also happens to be wrong.[10] So how is it that the Inquisition could have come up with the idea that Galileo was contradicting the scriptures? It seems that Galileo's critics were guilty of the same mistake which many of the present-day young-earth creationists have made. That is, they took the **plainest** reading of the scriptures as the "true" one and disallowed any alternate interpretations. For example, look at the Psalms:

"... In the heavens he has pitched a tent for the sun, ... It rises at one end of the heavens and makes its circuit to the other; ..."

— Psalm 19:4, 6.

This verse and many others such as, "The sun rose," in Genesis 32:31 were probably taken by the Inquisition to mean that it was the sun which moved across the sky not the earth's turning which caused day and night. The same argument can also be made from Joshua 10:13 which says, "So the sun stood still." In order for this to be an exception, the rule must be that the sun usually moves. Each of these verses speaks of the sun's daily motion across the sky in terms which imply motion of the sun rather than rotation of the earth. This would be the plainest reading of these verses. Still, it happens to be a wrong conclusion.

---

[9]The Sleepwalkers, Arthur Koestler, C. 1959, The Universal Library, Grosset and Dunlap, N.Y., P. 603.

[10]Actually modern cosmology provides a sort of defense for the Inquisition's position. According to the laws of relativity, any frame of reference can be taken as a stationary center of the universe. Of course this argument supports Galileo's position equally well.

These scriptural references are of a type often called "observer true." They are what appears to be true to an earth-bound observer. Even modern scientists will say things like, "The sun is going down." This is not really a "false" statement; it is simply the way this thought is expressed in our language. The writers of the Bible must be allowed at least as much freedom in their use of language as we give ourselves.

In this example, even though scientific theories and theological interpretations seemed to agree, both were wrong. As is now known, Galileo was correct – even though he was unable to scientifically prove his case to his inquisitors.[11] If he had not repented of his "heresy," he might have been burned at the stake as was Bruno before him. Whatever Galileo was, he was not a martyr. He compromised the truth in order to save the short remainder of his life.

Obviously, we must be very cautious. Even if our interpretation of scripture is in complete agreement with what scientists happen to believe at the present time, both understandings might be in error at the same time. When the evidence proves that we have been in error, we must be ready and willing to admit it; we must be honest. If we are unable to face up to our mistakes in this life, it will be difficult for us to stand before God and give an account of ourselves (Romans 14:10-12). This is especially important if our mistakes happen to present stumbling blocks to our brothers (Romans 14:13).

Conclusions

Science and theology are both fallible systems for seeking truth. God's Bible and His universe both supply unerring facts. Our own theories should be built upon the facts from both God's Bible and His creation. Even then, we must allow for the possibility that we might still be wrong. Perhaps the most important lesson we should learn from this is humility.

---

[11]Proof came in the mid-1800s in the form of the Foucalt pendulum and the detection of stellar parallax. See The Galileo Connection, by Charles E. Hummel, C. 1986, Inter Varsity Press, Downers Grove, Illinois, 60515, p. 111.

Chapter 3:
The Present-Day Stumbling Block

"Woe to the world because of *its* stumbling blocks! For it is inevitable that stumbling blocks come; but woe to that man through whom the stumbling block comes!"

—Matthew 18:7, N.A.S. Italics theirs.

The whole question concerning the age of the universe hangs on the length of the six creative "days" in the first chapter of Genesis. There the entire process of creation, from the heavens right down to man, is described as a sequence of six "days." This chapter will investigate some Biblical information concerning the length of those "days." More specifically, it will consider those arguments which are presented in support of the position that they must be six consecutive twenty-four-hour periods. Because nearly all scientists assure us that the events described within those six "days" covered a span of billions of years, we ought to examine the Biblical information very carefully.

Christians are often inclined to take the young-earth position simply because it appears to be the plainest reading of the Bible. In the first chapter, we learned why we should be more careful than this: Ancient writings, like Genesis, can be difficult to understand; the plainest reading may not necessarily be the correct one. God may actually have intended a meaning in Genesis which is different from the plain reading.

If the "days" in the first chapter of Genesis were longer than twenty-four hours in length, we might wonder why God chose a word (the Hebrew "yom" meaning "day") which would tend to hide the truth from men of our present day. He certainly would have realized this would cause complications. Would God knowingly allow people to miss the truth? Clearly, before even the soundest of arguments for the old-earth interpretation can be taken seriously, this question needs to be answered.

Is it possible that God might have worded His truth in a way which would hide it from people? Is there any scriptural evidence for this? As it turns out, there is. Consider the reason Jesus spoke in parables. There is no need to speculate about this because Jesus Himself explained the reason to His disciples in Matthew:

> "The knowledge of the secrets of the kingdom of heaven has been given to you, but not to them. Whoever has will be given more, and he will have an abundance. Whoever does not have, even what he has will be taken from him. **This is why I speak to them in parables**:
>
> "Though seeing, they do not see; though hearing, they do not hear or understand.
>
> "In them is fulfilled the prophecy of Isaiah:
>
> "'You will be ever hearing but never understanding; you will be ever seeing but never perceiving. For this people's heart has become calloused; they hardly hear with their ears, and **they have closed their eyes**. **Otherwise they might see with their eyes**, hear with their ears, understand with their hearts and turn, and I would heal them.'"
>
>   – Matthew 13:11-15, Emphasis mine.

This is an example of God, in scripture, intentionally hiding the truth from His own chosen people. God's reason, it appears, is to allow them to make their own choices. Those who do not want to see the truth do not have to see it.

Although God never lies,[1] it seems He does not always present His truth in the very plainest possible manner. God hides His messages in Biblical parables and buries His truths deeply in

---

[1]Numbers 23:19, Hebrews 6:17, 18, Titus 1:2

the earth's crust. Although we may have to keep our eyes open and search diligently to discover the truth, we will never find a lie in either God's Bible or His universe.

There is an important difference between hiding the truth and outright deception. God will never lie. Following God's example, parents should not lie to their children; but it is often a good idea to hide things from them — especially potentially dangerous things. Other times, rewards are hidden which are intended to be found; an Easter egg hunt is an example of this. Parents who hide Easter eggs often hide them differently for children of different ages. Younger children are given a head start. This is necessary if the hunt is to be fair to everyone.

There are different spiritual abilities too. The Jews had an advantage over the Gentiles in recognizing the Messiah. They were the ones who had studied the scriptures which spelled out exactly what the Messiah must be like (Psalm 22). They had been warned of the exact time of His coming (Daniel 9:25, 26). Paul refers to the advantages given them as being, "much in every way" (Romans 3:2). Yet Jesus was a "stumbling block" for them (1 Corinthians 1:23). Jesus presented Himself to them in a form which they found too hard to accept. Was it because God deliberately hid the truth from them? Paul says that it was:

"What Israel sought so earnestly it did not obtain, but the elect did. The others were hardened, as it is written:

"'God gave them a spirit of stupor, eyes so that they could not see and ears so that they could not hear, to this very day.'"

—Romans 11:7, 8.

Apparently this was deliberate. It looks like a case of God evening up people's chances.[2] For another example look at 1 Corinthians 1:26, 27:

"Brothers, think of what you were when you were called. Not many of you were wise by human standards; not many were influential; not many were of noble birth. But God chose the foolish things of the world to shame the

---

[2]See also 2 Corinthians 3:14, 15.

wise; God chose the weak things of the world to shame the strong. ..."

Here again we see God evening things up. He has chosen things which are foolish and weak to offset the advantages held by the wise and strong.

God hides things from the wise and intelligent and reveals them to little children (Luke 10:21). Fortunately, the wise and intelligent can find even hidden things if they are honestly looking for them. In Proverbs 25:2, Solomon tells us:

"It is the glory of God to conceal a matter; to search out a matter is the glory of kings."

God has concealed things for the wise (like Solomon's "kings") to search out; children are given the extra help they need. *Anyone* who seeks will find (Matthew 7:7, 8). God rewards those who earnestly seek Him (Hebrews 11:6). A lack of intelligence will not hinder a sincere seeker. On the other hand, if a man is not seeking God, his intelligence will not help him. Somehow, whether we are wise or simple, God's accessibility is always the same for us; but how is this possible? How can the weak and simple find God when the wise and strong are sometimes unable to?

God's methods of revelation accomplish this; He often reveals his truth in a manner which conceals it from the wise and strong. The mysteries of the kingdom are spoken in parables; the "stumbling block" keeps the Jews from having any obvious spiritual advantage over the Gentiles; and the foolishness of preaching prevents the wise from coming to Jesus if their spiritual condition warrants otherwise. With regard to fairness, concealment appears to be the rule rather than the exception.[3] Wise men are expected to see past it; little children are given help. This insures that access to God's kingdom depends on whether a man is sincerely seeking and not on his intelligence, education or strength.

Genesis 1 presents a situation where hiding truth might be necessary to balance different people's spiritual opportunities. If it had been written plainly, the large amount of accurate

---

[3]When God lays down moral law, on the other hand, He is very explicit.

scientific detail in that one short chapter would be overwhelming proof that Genesis was not written with mere human knowledge but by God Himself. Genesis describes discoveries which were not made until this century. Having this on the very first page of the Bible simply could not be ignored. Scientists would not be able to close their eyes and ears; they would be logically forced to become Christians.[4] Unfortunately, this would *not* be an advantage to those who did not have access to modern scientific knowledge. People who were less educated, or who simply were not born in this century, would find themselves at a spiritual disadvantage.

Because God sometimes arranges things to reduce unfairness, He might have *intentionally* concealed the evidence in Genesis 1 from modern scientists by using archaic and cryptic language. Although there are other methods God might have used, this is certainly a possibility. Because scientific knowledge *has* increased, God might have used a "stumbling block" to insure that scientists do not gain an advantage over the rest of us. The apparent "foolishness" of the term "day" in the first chapter of Genesis could easily be because of this.

At this point, some readers might be wondering why *Christians* seem to be misled by God's term "day" while scientists − even those who are atheists − are allowed to see the truth about the age of the universe. Although this might appear to be backwards, it really is not; remember, this camouflage has been applied to the Bible, not to the universe. What is really the issue in God's eyes is not who knows how old the universe is and who doesn't − but who has believed His word and has received His son Jesus as savior and who hasn't. Here, where it really matters, the Christians (including those creationists who err concerning the earth's age) have *not* been blinded by the wording of Genesis 1 while the atheists (including those scientists who know correctly the earth's age) have been blinded. It is exactly this spiritual condition which the blinding is aimed at − not the specific dates and ages.

Now that we understand why God might have worded Genesis in a way which could confound even the wise, we will

---

[4]If the New Testament were not also accepted, they would at least be forced to become Jews.

be more inclined to evaluate young-earth arguments with adequate caution. The following seven arguments have been given by young-earth creationists for why the Genesis "days" *must* be six consecutive twenty-four hour periods.[5]

Arguments for 24-hour days:

1) That the twenty-four-hour interpretation is the most literal reading of the text; God should have used alternate wording if He had intended the "age" interpretation.

2) That Genesis 1:14 forces the twenty-four-hour interpretation by using "yom" (the Hebrew word for "day") in a context which excludes the "age" possibility.

3) That the use of the expression "evening and morning" forces the twenty-four-hour interpretation.

4) That the use of a number appended to the word "day" forces the twenty-four-hour interpretation.

5) That the twenty-four-hour interpretation is forced by the reference to Genesis 1 from Exodus 20:9-11, where our work week is explained.

6) That the "age" interpretation must be wrong since it carries a consequence that death must have preceded sin and the fall.

7) That the "age" interpretation is merely to accommodate the evolutionists.

---

[5]Some additional arguments which merely allow for this possibility will be dealt with in the next chapter.

These are typical of arguments given in support of the young-earth position; they are intended to be representative of the best arguments given. Their full text is provided in Appendix 2 so readers may examine these arguments in their original context.

Although this appears to be an impressive battery, each of these arguments contains at least one fatal flaw. This will be seen as they are examined one at a time. We must remember that these are all just theological **theories** designed by fallible men. Not one of them is actual scripture. Theories can never be proven true; but each of these will be proved false as it is examined in detail.

Argument #1

> That the twenty-four-hour interpretation is the most literal reading of the text; God should have used alternate wording if He had intended the "age" interpretation.

This certainly seems true. Although the Hebrew word for day "yom" can also refer to an indefinite period of time, this is not obvious to an English reader today; but, as we have seen, this is what we might expect even if the "age" interpretation is the correct one. God sometimes hides truth from the wise and Genesis 1 is a natural target for this; there is a need to be fair to nonscientists. In any case, Genesis is an extremely ancient writing; it was not originally written in **plain English** and is likely to be difficult to understand.

Even so, the actual text must tell the truth; furthermore, we ought to be able to see it if we are honestly looking for it. Because scriptural authority must *not* be compromised, only the **literal** interpretations will be accepted here. **Spiritual, symbolic** or **figurative** interpretations will be rejected. While it is true that the twenty-four-hour sense of the word "yom" is far more common than the "age" sense, the "age" meaning is still a **literal** rendering of "yom." It is *not* **spiritual, symbolic** or **figurative**. This was seen in the previous chapter from the parallel between the ancient Hebrew "yom" and the modern English "day." Also, "day" was used this way in Genesis 2:17. The twenty-four-hour and "age" interpretations are both **literal**. Although the twenty-four-hour meaning for "yom" is more common or more **plain reading**, it is not really more **literal** than the "age" meaning.

Argument #1, for the twenty-four-hour interpretation, does not hold up under strict inspection. The decision on the length of the Genesis "days" should be made on some other basis.

Argument #2

That Genesis 1:14 forces the twenty-four-hour interpretation by using "yom" in a context which excludes the "age" possibility.

This argument says that since the word "days"[6] in verse 14 is used in a context which can only mean a sequence of twenty-four-hour periods, other usages of the word "day" in the same passage must follow suit and also refer to twenty-four-hour periods.[7]

The use of the same word in a closely related passage is a good general rule of interpretation; but this rule must *not* be applied carelessly. Because the word "day" is used many times in this passage, *all* of the usages should be considered to get the whole picture – not just one from verse 14.

In the first two chapters,[8] where the "days" in question are found, the word "day" occurs fifteen times and the word "days" once. The single occurrence of the word "days" carries the twenty-four-hour meaning. Of the remaining fifteen usages, nine refer to the days of creation themselves. No assumptions can be made about them because that would be "begging the question."[9]

---

[6]"Days" is "yamim" in Hebrew which is simply the plural of "yom."

[7]Actually, the only occurrence of "day" (singular) in verse 14 refers to the 12 daylight hours as opposed to night. Only the plural occurrence "days" refers to 24-hour periods.

[8]Counting was deliberately suspended at the end of the second chapter. This is because the serpent used the word "day" when he misrepresented God in the third chapter. It is quite possible that he used it differently than God did originally. The serpent's usage would have only contaminated the statistics.

[9]"Begging the Question," means assuming in advance a conclusion to a particular problem, then using that assumption as data to help determine the solution. This is a form of circular reasoning.

Of the remaining six, the context forces the twelve-hour daylight meaning (as opposed to night) four times and a greater-than-twenty-four-hour meaning twice.[10]

Because "day" is used so many different ways, this rule gives different results depending upon how it is applied. There are three different possible meanings for "day" used in the surrounding context. Obviously, this rule is not infallible.[11] After all, it is not scripture itself, just a fallible human **theory** about scripture. Again, the decision about the length of the creative days must be made on some other basis.

Argument #3

That the use of the Hebrew expression "evening and morning" forces the twenty-four-hour interpretation.

This argument is presented as if it were a general rule of interpreting scripture; but no reason is provided as to why it should be considered a valid one – especially considering the antiquity of the text. Like the word "day" the Hebrew words for "evening" and "morning" ("arab" and "boqer") both have multiple definitions. It can be seen from Psalm 90:14 that "Morning" carries a meaning which is *not* tied to a twenty-four-hour day:

"O satisfy us **early** with thy mercy; that we may rejoice and be glad all our days."

–K.J.V. Emphasis mine.

---

[10]Genesis 2:4 uses "yom" (singular) in a context which is usually taken to refer back to several of the creative days. Genesis 2:17, as we have seen, is the "day" in which Adam died.

[11]This rule also fails for Matthew 8:22. There Jesus said, "Follow me, and let the dead bury their own dead." The same word "dead" (nekros in the original New Testament Greek) is used twice in this verse and must mean **spiritually** dead the first time and **physically** dead the second time. Otherwise we either have corpses burying the dead or living people being buried.

Here, the Hebrew word "boqer" (emphasized word) was translated as "early" rather than "in the morning" because it was obvious from context that "in the early part of a person's lifetime" rather than "in the morning of a particular twenty-four-hour period" was what the Psalmist had intended; otherwise, whether the blessing came in the morning or the evening would have very little to do with how much time would remain for rejoicing during that person's lifetime.[12]

But what about when "evening and morning" appear together as argument #3 requires? Psalm 90:14 does not exactly apply because "evening" and "morning" are not both used there. "Evening" and "morning" occur together many places in the Bible. In the first chapter of Genesis, this happens six times. Other usages are: Exodus 18:13, 14 & 27:21; Leviticus 24:3; Numbers 9:21; 1 Samuel 17:16;[13] 1 Chron. 16:40; 2 Chron. 2:4 & 31:3; Ezra 3:3; Job 4:20; Psalm 55:17 and Daniel 8:26. As can be seen from examining context of these verses, the expression usually carries the idea of "continuously." For example, instruction may be given to do something "evening and morning." Not only is the thing to be done in the evening and in the morning, but it is also understood that it is to be done day after day. The Living Bible renders the expression "Day and night" in Exodus 27:21. Other acceptable paraphrasings might be "day after day" or even "around the clock" in some cases.

At first glance, the sense of "continuously" does not seem to fit into the context of Genesis 1 no matter which interpretation is assigned to the six days; but it is possible that this phrase is telling us that each of God's creative acts merely commenced on the particular day named and then continued during subsequent days. If this were the case, either interpretation ("age" or twenty-four-hour) would fit equally well.

None of the usages of evening and morning appear to limit an event to just twenty-four hours. Job 4:20 speaks figuratively of men's "houses" of clay which are destroyed between "morning and evening." This process seems slow to men but not

---

[12]This is a literal usage. For comparison, see the figurative usage of evening and morning at Psalm 90:5-6.

[13]Here the word for morning is shakam.

to God. Daniel 8:26 relates a vision of Daniel's which covered future dynasties of man up until the end time.

"And the vision of the evening and the morning which was told *is* true: wherefore shut thou up the vision; for it *shall be* for many days."

— Daniel 8:26, K.J.V. Italics theirs.

Here the expression "evening and morning" appears to mean something like "from beginning to end" — the entire rule of man. The translators of both the N.I.V. and N.A.S. Bibles rendered the phrase as "evenings and mornings" — apparently to make the greater-than-twenty-four-hour meaning more clear to modern readers. ("Evening" and "morning" are both singular in the Hebrew.) Daniel seems to confirm the greater-than-twenty-four-hour meaning, but the confirmation is weak; Genesis and Daniel represent very different times and cultures.[14]

In any case, the presence of the expression "evening and morning" does not by itself establish that the "days" of creation were twenty-four hours in length. It would seem there is still no clear way to decide how to interpret the word "day." As before, the decision should be made on some other basis.

Argument #4

That the use of a number appended to the word "day" forces the twenty-four-hour interpretation.

Like argument #3, this argument is also presented as if it were a general rule of interpretation. The problem with this is there is no reason why God should only be permitted to number twenty-four-hour periods of time. It will be shown from scripture that the use of a number appended to the word "day" can sometimes refer to a greater-than-twenty-four-hour period.

---

[14]Daniel 8:26 was written in Hebrew and is therefore at least partially parallel to Genesis. It has not been overlooked that other chapters in Daniel (chapters three through seven and also most of chapter two) were originally written in Aramaic. See the note in The New Scofield Reference Edition Bible, for Daniel 2:4.

Consider the "last" day. Although "last" is not strictly a number, it is certainly grammatically analogous to "first" and hence must be given consideration here. Isaiah 30:8 reads:

"... That it may serve in the time to come
As a witness forever."

                                    —N.A.S.

The phrase "in the time to come" has been translated from two Hebrew words meaning "for the day" and "latter"[15] – or in other words, "for the last day." This translator (N.A.S.) rendered "day" as "time" because it is obvious from context that an indefinite period is what was intended. This should not be a surprise to anyone. The N.I.V. translated "yom" singular as "days" plural here. The effect is the same.

For another example, the number "one" appended to the word "day" can also refer to a daylight period of indefinite length. Zechariah 14:7 says:

"But it shall be **one day** which shall be known to the Lord, not day, nor night; but it shall come to pass, *that* at evening time it shall be light."

                    —K.J.V. Emphasis mine, italics theirs.

This is a description of the new Jerusalem in which there will be no night (Revelation 22:5). Notice that in this verse, the one single "day" (daylight period) is understood to last for a long indefinite period of time. Here the phrase "one day" and back in Genesis 1:5 the phrase "the first day" are both translated from the exact same Hebrew phrase "yom echad."

God is certainly as free to number indefinite periods of time as He is to number twenty-four-hour ones. Days two through seven deserve parallel treatment for this reason.

Argument #4 is inconclusive. The rule of "a number appended to the word 'day'" can be used against the twenty-four-hour interpretation as well as for it; parallel applications of the rule speak of long "days." It appears that the numbers appended to the "days" in Genesis prove nothing at all about the length or

---

[15]See Isaiah 30:8 The Interlinear Bible, Jay P. Green Sr., C. 1976, 1979, Baker Book House, Grand Rapids, Michigan, p. 556.

meaning of those days. Again, the decision must be made on some other basis.

Argument #5

That the twenty-four-hour interpretation is forced by the reference to Genesis 1 from Exodus 20:9-11, where our work week is explained.

In Exodus 20:9-11, God gives the reason for our six days of work to one day of rest schedule:

"Six days you shall labor and do all your work, but the seventh day is a Sabbath to the Lord your God. On it you shall not do any work, ... For in six days the Lord made the heavens and the earth, the sea, and all that is in them, but he rested on the seventh day."

Because our days are twenty-four-hour days and because they are modeled after God's, it would seem to follow that God's days must have been twenty-four-hour ones also; but there is more information which must also be taken into account. Leviticus 25:3, 4 says:

"For six years sow your fields, ... But in the seventh year the land is to have a sabbath of rest, ..."

Although it doesn't specifically so state, it is clear that this was also modeled after God's work week. It cannot also follow that God's "days" were 365-day years. Likewise it does not really follow from our work week that God's "days" were twenty-four hours long.

What argument #5 is doing wrong is confusing the object with its shadow. Many things in the Bible are merely shadows of greater heavenly truths. Paul referred to this in Colossians 2:16, 17:

"Therefore do not let anyone judge you by what you eat or drink, or with regard to a religious festival, a New Moon celebration or a Sabbath day. These are a shadow of the things that were to come; the reality, however, is found in Christ."

This is also seen in Hebrews 8:5:

"They serve at a sanctuary that is a copy and shadow of what is in heaven."

Both our work week and the work "week" of our fields are shadows of God's work "week." His week was not modeled after ours but ours after His. It is never very safe to make absolute conclusions about the nature of an object by merely looking at its shadow. God's work week has cast shadows of two different lengths – six days and six years. Nothing can be determined from this about the length of God's week. The only common denominator seems to be the 6:1 work to rest ratio.

Notice also what Hebrews says:

"For somewhere he has spoken about the seventh day in these words: 'And on the seventh day God rested from all his work.' And again in the passage above he says, 'They shall never enter my rest.' It still remains that some will enter **that rest**, ... There remains, then, a Sabbath-rest for the people of God; for anyone who enters God's rest also rests from his own work, just as God [did] from his."

– Hebrews 4:4-10, Emphasis and brackets mine.

(The bracketed word is not present in the original Greek of the New Testament.[16])

Here it sounds very much as if God's Sabbath rest is still in progress and is the same rest[17] that we are to enter into.[18] It would seem that at least God's seventh day is longer than twenty-four hours. If God's day of rest is still in progress, then

---

[16]*The Interlinear Greek-English New Testament*, Rev. Alfred Marshall D.Litt., C. 1958, Zondervan Publishing House, Grand Rapids, Michigan, p. 861. It is my belief that, "as God *is doing* from his," would be a more correct paraphrasing of this verse.

[17]The phrase "that rest," is translated from a pronoun in the Greek text which clearly refers back to God's rest.

[18]The idea that God's seventh-day rest is still in progress fits with the rest of scripture where this is mentioned. Jesus said, "My father is always at his work to this very day, and I, too, am working." (John 5:17). This was to justify His act of having healed an invalid man on the Sabbath. Notice here that Jesus' argument would make sense however one interprets the duration of God's Sabbath; in either case it is understood that God is working during His Sabbath.

there appears to be a reason why the description for the seventh day in Genesis 2:2, 3 does not end with the expected concluding expression, "evening and morning – the seventh day"; the seventh day itself would not yet have seen its conclusion. If the seven days were all twenty-four hours long, this omission would be difficult to understand.

Because argument #5 is based on a mere shadow, it is therefore a very weak argument. It certainly would not stand against any physical evidence to the contrary. In fact, as we have seen, there is even some scriptural indication that God's Sabbath day is still in progress. The final decision about the length of the creative days must *not* be based on this argument either.

Argument #6

That the "age" interpretation must be wrong since it carries a consequence that death must have preceded sin and the fall.

The "age" interpretation does disagree with some traditional beliefs concerning the fall. According to the fossil evidence, the dinosaurs became extinct more than sixty million years before man was created. This means they must have died before Adam's fall. Furthermore, there is scientific evidence that many creatures, from before the time of men, ate other animals.[19] The evidence says there *was* animal death before Adam.

Although this disagrees with a popular scriptural **theory**, it is *not* in disagreement with scripture itself. Scripture gives no reason why animals couldn't have died before Adam's sin. Adam was told that he would die as a result of his own sin. Paul points out that men who lived between Adam and Moses also died as a result of Adam's sin; but nowhere does the Bible say that *animals* die as a consequence of human sin.[20] (Of course those

---

[19]For example, the fossilized skeletal remains exist of a large fish from the Cretaceous period (long before man appeared) which had swallowed whole a smaller fish of a different species. See, The Cambridge Encyclopedia of Earth Sciences, Ed. David G. Smith, C. 1981, Crown Publishers Inc. / Cambridge University Press, N.Y., p. 369.

[20]It is possible to interpret Romans 8:19-22 to disagree with this statement; but it is clear that God's angels are an exception here as they are not under the

particular animals which were sacrificed as a sin offering are excepted.)

In support of Argument #6, young-earth creationists often cite Romans 5:12:

"... just as sin entered the world through one man, and death through sin, and in this way death came to **all men**, because all sinned-."

Emphasis mine

This tells us that *human* death entered through Adam's sin but says nothing specifically about animal or plant death. This verse does not say *all* death entered the world through sin any more than Genesis says Eve gave birth to animals as well as men:

"Adam named his wife Eve, because she would become the mother of **all the living**."

– Genesis 3:20, Emphasis mine.

Clearly "all the living" refers only to humans. Insisting on the *very plainest* reading often violates simple common sense. Because Paul specifically said death came to "all men," it is unreasonable to insist that he intended more than that.

Presumably, anyone who believes that animals did not die before Adam sinned must believe that up until that time carnivores ate plants in the same manner that, "a lion shall eat straw like the ox,"[21] during the millennium (Isaiah 11:7). Even so, there must have been some form of death before Adam's fall. At the very least some parts of plants must have "died" to feed those animals. It is therefore plain that at least some form of

---

"bondage of corruption." Because we must allow for at least this exception, we are unjustified in insisting that animals are included here; they could easily be another exception.

[21] As Christians we should have no trouble accepting the reality of this prophecy. God *does* work miracles. We are assured that one day the lion *will* eat straw like the ox even though we do not see it happening today. Also, the garden of Eden was a very special place – different in many ways from the rest of the world. While Adam was in the garden, he did not have to cope with thorns and thistles which probably were already created and waiting for him just outside the circle of God's protection (Genesis 3:18).

plant death was in the world before Adam sinned.[22] It follows that when Paul said that death entered through sin, he could not possibly have meant *all* death.

In fact, there was even a *man* who lived and died after Adam yet was not under the curse of sin and death at all; Jesus was that exception. Consider what it was about Him that made Him acceptable as a sacrifice for our sins when no other human would do. The answer is, of course, that He was not guilty of sin; neither was He under its curse (Hebrews 4:15, 1 John 3:5). Only a man who had no sin, original or personal, would be properly qualified.

Now, if "all men" inherited Adam's original fallen nature, how is it that Jesus escaped this curse? Even those men who lived between Adam and Moses – those who had broken *no* specific law themselves – were under the curse of sin and owed the same price which Adam had to pay! None of them transgressed; yet they all died. Why was Jesus' death a sacrifice and not merely payment due?

One possibility stems from the fact that Jesus had no human father even though He did have a human mother. According to this theory, we somehow inherit original sin through our father's bloodline.[23] Another possibility is that God miraculously intervened and thus severed the connection to Adam's sin. Were it not for some such explanation, Jesus would have inherited Adam's original sin and could not have been "without sin" as the Bible establishes that He was. This seems to be why Adam's sin nature, and its inevitable consequence, was not passed on to Jesus as it was to everyone else; one way or another, Jesus was not entirely connected to Adam's lineage.

Now what about animals? Is there any possible way that they could have inherited Adam's sin nature? Of course not! They are

---

[22]Of course there is no blood involved in the case of plants – see Hebrews 9:22 – but see the next argument concerning Jesus. Also, if animals were able to digest plants, this means that at least some laws governing decomposition (decay) were in effect at that time. This means the second law of thermodynamics must have worked then just as it does now; life itself depends on this law.

[23]If this inheritance were physical, the laws of genetics predict that only males would inherit Adam's sin. Because we believe otherwise, we must conclude that this would be strictly a spiritual inheritance.

not connected to Adam's bloodline in any way whatsoever. Therefore, they cannot be included with us in our fallen state. This is probably why they could be used for the Old Testament sacrifices; they were innocent.

Apparently, present-day animals are not under the curse of Adam's sin; yet they still die physically. It follows that animal death is not a result of Adam's sin. Animals would be dying even if Adam had not sinned. Ancient animals, which preceded Adam's fall, would also have died. This difference between Adam and the animals – that he might not have died while they would have in any case – was probably a result of Adam having been created in the image of God (Genesis 1:27) while the animals were not.

So argument #6, like arguments #1 through #5, also fails to throw the case in favor of the twenty-four-hour interpretation. Although the old-earth creationist's position carries the consequence that animal death must have preceded Adam's sin, this argument does not eliminate the old-earth position as a possibility. There really is no Biblical reason why animals could not have died before Adam's fall. Once again, the decision must be made on some other basis.

Argument #7

That the "age interpretation" is merely to accommodate the evolutionists.

This author is an old-earth creationist, *not* an evolutionist. He has no desire to accommodate any error – not even that of his fellow creationists. Argument #7 is not applicable in this case; and in any case, decisions should always be founded on the actual evidence – not on the biases or motives (real or imagined) of the various individuals who happen to hold the different positions.

This argument also encounters a difficulty with history. The realization that the earth is old came many years *before* Darwin's theory.[24] Therefore, it could not possibly have been an attempt to accommodate evolution in any way whatsoever.

One Last Argument

Each of the arguments for the twenty-four-hour-day position has been examined and found to be inconclusive at best. Some of them even suggest the "days" were longer than twenty-four hours. There seems to be *no* scriptural proof that the "days" of Genesis were consecutive twenty-four-hour periods. If there is any such proof, this author has not seen it; but there *is* proof that those days were *not* consecutive twenty-four hour periods.

The Bible is truth; but God has written other truth as well. The universe is also God's work. The very same God who created the Bible also created the physical universe. God does not lie – *ever*. The Bible is quite clear about that.[25] He did not lie during the thousands of years when He was "writing" the Bible. He did not lie as He "wrote" the universe either.

In case there is any doubt, we are told in the Bible that we see truth when we study God's universe:

"The heavens declare the glory of God; the skies proclaim the work of his hands. Day after day they pour forth speech; night after night they display knowledge."

–Psalm 19:1, 2.

The Bible even tells us we can learn spiritual truth from God's creation:

"God's invisible qualities – his eternal power and divine nature – have been clearly seen, being understood from what has been made..."

–Romans 1:20.

---

[24]The old-earth position was originally proposed by James Hutton during the late 1700's. Darwin's theory came during the late 1800's. Interestingly, Hutton believed God had created the world and would eventually destroy it. Hen's Teeth and Horse's Toes, Stephen J. Gould, C. 1983, W.W. Norton & Co., N.Y., pp. 84, 85.

[25]Numbers 23:19, Hebrews 6:17, 18, Titus 1:2

The Bible is God's word and should be taken to mean exactly what it says – literally! How should the universe be read? It has the same author. There is certainly no reason to assume that it should be taken differently than the Bible; God's universe deserves the same *literal* reading.

It is difficult to interpret the heavens and the earth correctly. Throughout history men have made many mistakes trying. This does not mean the universe itself cannot be trusted as a source of truth. As is well known, men have made just as many mistakes trying to interpret the Bible; yet the Bible itself can certainly be trusted! In either case, the true reading will not always be the "plainest;" but there will be no lies included in the actual "text."

The hard evidence for a very old earth is real. This will become clear in the following chapters as some of the most misunderstood aspects of God's other "book" – the universe – are explored.

There will be stumbling blocks. Jesus said in Matthew 18:7 this was inevitable. However, our responsibility as Christians is to make sure that we do not put them there; there will be "Woe" to those who do! The "days" of Genesis 1 appear to present such stumbling blocks. It is most important that we are *not* responsible for magnifying these obstacles when we talk to non-Christians. We must not make our preaching more foolish than it absolutely needs to be. There is already *enough* hindrance in the world to keep scientists from finding their way to Christ without our making it worse!

Chapter 4:
Missing the Obvious

"The heavens declare the glory of God; the skies proclaim the work of his hands. Day after day they pour forth speech; night after night they display knowledge."

−Psalms 19:1, 2.

The universe was only created once. There were not two separate creations − one for the information in the first chapter of Genesis and another for the information seen through telescopes. It follows that there should be no contradictions between the two accounts.

God's universe demands a literal reading just like His Bible does. God's word, in Psalm 19:1, 2 (quoted above), explains that His creation speaks the truth. Ironically, those Christians who are most insistent that we take the plainest meaning of every word in the Bible often miss the most obvious reading of God's heavens. They are correct that God's Bible speaks the truth; but so do His heavens. God's word ought to be trusted without disregarding the scientific reading of His creation. What is needed is a proper regard for both.

God's invisible qualities, such as His unfathomable timelessness, are written all over His heavens. As explained in previous chapters, the Bible even tells us to expect the heavens to reflect God's eternal nature:

"God's invisible qualities – his **eternal** power and divine nature – have been clearly seen, being understood from what has been made ... "

– Romans 1:20, Emphasis mine.

When atheistic scientists read the heavens, they see an agelessness about them even when they fail to see something as obvious as the creation's need for a creator. When young-earth creationists read the heavens they appear almost as blind as the atheistic scientists; they appear to be blinded to the incomprehensible age of the creation. It would seem that, of all people, it should be the Christians who would be able to see a "shadow" of God's eternal nature proclaimed in the heavens.

The universe *is very old*; exactly *how old* is not really known. Present estimates run in the fifteen-to-twenty-billion-year range but even the scientists have not settled on an exact age. Only God really knows. Here it will be demonstrated that the universe is much older than the twenty-four-hour interpretation of Genesis allows for. One of the simplest proofs is a consequence of the size of the universe and the speed of light.

If there is anything about the heavens which is usually agreed upon by creationist and evolutionist alike, it is that they are extremely large. We all have some concept of how large the Earth must be; but it is difficult to fathom the 238,854 mile distance to the Moon.[1] When we look at it at night, it is very hard to imagine that it is 2160 miles in diameter and so very far away. Still, relatively speaking, the moon is very close to us. The closest planets, Mars and Venus, never come nearly as close. The Sun is a staggering 92,900,000 miles away from us. This is just as well; every second it unleashes trillions of times as much energy as the Hiroshima bomb. Even at our tremendous distance, a person can still get "burned by the Sun."

The Sun is very far from us; but the Sun, the Moon, the Earth and all the other planets sit together in a little group all alone by themselves in a giant sea of empty space. The stars are

---

[1]Handbook of Chemistry and Physics 49th Edition, Ed. Robert C. Weast, Ph.D., C. 1964, The Chemical Rubber Company, Cleveland, Ohio, pp. F-144, 145. This is the source for all of the astronomical distances and diameters presented in this chapter. (Distances are center-to-center averages.)

not even close to them. In fact, the entire 92,900,000 miles between the Earth and the Sun would completely disappear if it were viewed from even the closest star. And the closest star would scarcely appear distinct from the Sun if it were viewed from even the closest of galaxies. (A galaxy is a cluster of millions or even billions of stars). And individual galaxies are virtually lost in the sea of the universe's superclusters. (Superclusters are large clusters made up of smaller clusters – which, in turn, each contain hundreds or thousands of individual galaxies.)[2] The universe is even larger than a supercluster. How much larger? Like its age, no one has yet figured out exactly how large the universe really is either.

The mere fact that distant stars can be seen proves that they were there a very long time ago. Light travels very rapidly – 186,282 miles in a single second; but even at that speed, light has to have been traveling for more than two million years to reach us from even our closest neighboring spiral galaxy[3] which is located in the constellation Andromeda and identified simply as "M31."[4] M31 is *that* far away from us!

If M31 were younger than two million years, light from it would not have had time to reach us; this means we would not even know there was an M31 galaxy. The light would still be in space somewhere in between it and us – still rushing toward us. But the light has already arrived here from M31 and we *do* see it. So how old is M31? Anyone who suggests that it is less than two million years old is simply disregarding the evidence. The only **literal** reading of God's universe is that we see M31 because light has traveled from it to us, and that takes time!

M31 is far away; but compared to other things in God's universe, it is relatively close. Light from objects, which are greatly more distant, shows that the universe is older still; light takes more than 300 million years to reach us from the Coma-

---

[2]"Superclusters and Voids in the Distribution of Galaxies," by Stephen A. Gregory and Laird A. Thompson, SCIENTIFIC AMERICAN, March 1982, Vol. 246, No. 3, p. 106.

[3]Mysteries of the Universe, Nigel Henbest, C. 1981, Van Nostrand Reinhold Company, N.Y., pp. 171-172.

[4]M31 is also called NGC 224 in the "New General Catalog." Because it is located in the constellation Andromeda, M31 is sometimes also called the "Andromeda Galaxy."

A1367 supercluster[5] and many billions of years to reach us from the most distant quasars.[6]

In spite of this scientific evidence, there are still a great many creationists who hold that God created the universe about ten thousand years ago. The three following explanations are usually offered in defense of this position.

Explanations for Visible Starlight in a Young Universe

1) That the stars are actually very close to us and are very small.
2) That light used to travel more quickly in the past than it does today.
3) That God created the light in transit between the stars and us.

Explanation #1

That the stars are very close to us

When this explanation is even mentioned at all, it is not usually taken seriously. It is normally included as another logical possibility – but one which is not considered to be very likely.[7] After all, the astronomers were right about the distances to the Moon, Venus, Mercury, Mars, Jupiter, Saturn, Uranus and Neptune. We know – we've sent spacecraft to them. Why should

---

[5] "Superclusters and Voids in the Distribution of Galaxies," by Stephen A. Gregory and Laird A Thompson, SCIENTIFIC AMERICAN, March 1982, Vol. 246, No. 3, p. 114.

[6] "Quasars as Probes of the Distant and Early Universe," by Patrick S. Osmer, SCIENTIFIC AMERICAN, February 1982, Vol. 246, No. 2, p. 126.

[7] This actually appears to be suggested as a serious alternative in Science and Creation, by William W Boardman Jr. Robert F. Koontz, and Henry M. Morris, C. 1973, Creation-Science Research Center, San Diego, California, p. 26.

astronomers suddenly be wrong – and so very wrong too – only when they start to measure the distances to the stars?

The M31 galaxy will make a good enough example to refute explanation #1, even though there are other objects in the universe which are thousands of times farther away from us than it is. If M31 were close enough to be seen in a 10,000-year-old universe, then it would have to be within 10,000 light-years of planet Earth. (A light-year is not a unit of time but the *distance* light travels in a year.)[8] This means it would be 200 times closer to us than the astronomers say. Even this assumption would mean that M31 had been invisible for the first 10,000 years of the universe's existence; and anything more distant than it would still be invisible for ages yet to come.

Of course, if a star is closer it will also appear brighter to an observer here on earth. According to the inverse square law of light intensity,[9] a star which is 200 times closer should appear 40,000 times brighter. This means that if the stars in the M31 galaxy were 200 times closer, they would also have to be 40,000 times dimmer than expected if they are going to appear to us as dimly as they do.

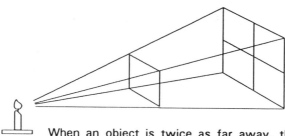

When an object is twice as far away, the same amount of light must cover four times the area. The area which the light must cover increases as the square of the distance.

A particular class of stars called Cepheid variables proves that stars in M31 are not dimmer than expected. These stars

---

[8] A light-year is about six trillion miles.

[9] A Second Course of Light, A.E.E. McKenzie M.A., 1956, reprinted 1965, Cambridge University Press, Great Britain, p. 166.

pulse at a rate which is linked to their absolute brightness. By merely watching their pulse rates, astronomers can know how bright these stars actually are. For this reason, it is clear that the Cepheid variable stars in the M31 galaxy are not dimmer and closer than astronomers say.[10]

Explanation #2

That light used to travel faster in the past

Perhaps the best exposition of this idea has been done by Trevor Norman and Barry Setterfield.[11] Their explanation not only attempts to explain how distant stars can be seen, it also attempts to explain a few other supposedly related phenomena such as radioactive dating. Although this explanation also fails as a viable alternative to an old universe, it is still quite interesting. There is much to be learned about scientific inquiry from studying it closely.

In its outward appearance, the theory is supported by actual measurements which have been made of the speed of light over the past few hundred years. A curve has been fit reasonably well through these measurements – one which, when greatly extrapolated, indicates that the speed of light was extremely fast about six thousand years ago[12] – fast enough to allow for the most distant stars to be visible in a young universe.

---

[10]Mysteries of the Universe, by Nigel Henbest, C. 1981, Van Nostrand Reinhold Co., N.Y., pp. 91, 170.

[11]The Atomic Constants, Light, and Time, by Trevor Norman and Barry Setterfield, C. 1987, Stanford Research Institute International, 333 Ravenswood Ave. Menlo Park, Ca. 94025. Creationists usually reject theories, such as this one, which appeal to changes in the physical constants. It is believed that God must have chosen those constants very carefully for the universe to function correctly. For example, it is cited that, "the hydrogen atom could not exist if the mass of the proton was just .2% greater (De Young, 1985)." See, "Has the Speed of Light Decayed?" By Gerald E. Aardsma, Ph.D. Institute for Creation Research, San Diego, Ca., I.C.R. Technical Report No. 1187, p. 1.

[12]Their data showed a maximum change of less than 1/2 percent over the past 250 years, Ibid p. 26. This change was approximately equal to the measuring error. From this Setterfield has extrapolated that the speed of light 6000 years ago was many millions of times its present value. See Geological Time and

The claim is that the speed of light has been decreasing with time. Because the speed of light, in a vacuum and in the absence of a strong gravitational field, is so perfectly constant no matter how or where it is measured, Norman and Setterfield have added the restriction that the speed of light is the same everywhere in the universe at any given instant; they claim it varies everywhere at the same rate.[13] This is an attempt to reconcile this theory with Einstein's theory of relativity. What relativity has to say about this will be considered later; but first the data will be examined.

Ever since man realized that light did not travel instantaneously from one place to another, he has been trying to measure its speed. The first attempts were more crude than modern ones because of the limitations imposed by the available equipment; but as instrumentation improved, so did the measurements. At present the figure is known quite precisely to be 299,792,458 meters per second (to within some fraction of a meter); but the first approximate measurements of centuries past were a fraction of a percent higher.

What is interesting here is that after the first few rough measurements were made, it appears that other scientists tended to be influenced by these early measurements. As a consequence, the accepted value approached the correct value more or less from one side,[14] instead of bouncing back and forth randomly between too fast and too slow quite as much as one might have expected if measuring error were truly random. Measuring error is seldom random. Scientists are people and people have expectations. The direction of experimental error is almost invariably influenced by these expectations. Even the best scientists are slightly inclined to discover what they expect to discover instead of what is really the truth.

Scriptural Chronology, Barry Setterfield, Box 318, Blackwood, S.A., 5051 Australia, pp. 1, 7.

[13]The Atomic Constants, Light, and Time, by Trevor Norman and Barry Setterfield, C. 1987, Stanford Research Institute International, 333 Ravenswood Ave. Menlo Park, Ca. 94025, pp. 9, 84.

[14]This effect is not uncommon in scientific inquiry. See, "Has the Speed of Light Decayed?" By Gerald E. Aardsma, Ph.D. Institute for Creation Research, San Diego, Ca., I.C.R. Technical Report No. 1187, p. 2.

The Norman/Setterfield Speed of Light Data[15]

Date	Measured Value	Estimated Error	(Real Error)
1740	300,650,000	?	860,000
1783	300,460,000	160,000	670,000
1843	300,020,000	160,000	230,000
1861	300,050,000	?	260,000
1874	299,990,000	200,000	200,000
1874	299,900,000	200,000	110,000
1876	299,921,000	13,000	130,000
1879	299,910,000	50,000	120,000
1882	299,860,000	30,000	70,000
1882	299,853,000	60,000	60,000
1883	299,850,000	90,000	60,000
1900	299,900,000	80,000	110,000
1902	299,860,000	80,000	70,000
1902	299,901,000	84,000	110,000
1906	299,803,000	30,000	10,500
1923	299,795,000	30,000	2500
1924	299,802,000	30,000	9500
1926	299,798,000	15,000	5500
1928	299,786,000	10,000	-6500
1932	299,774,000	10,000	-18,500
1936	299,771,000	10,000	-21,500
1937	299,771,000	10,000	-21,500
1940	299,776,000	10,000	-16,500
1947	299,798,000	3000	5500
1947	299,792,000	3000	-460
1949	299,792,400	2400	-60
1949	299,796,000	2000	3500
1950	299,792,500	1000	40
1950	299,794,300	1200	1840
1950	299,793,100	260	640
1951	299,793,100	400	640
1951	299,794,200	1400	1740
1951	299,792,600	700	140
1953	299,792,850	160	390
1954	299,792,750	300	290
1954	299,795,100	3100	2640
1955	299,792,400	400	-60
1955	299,792,000	6000	-460
1956	299,792,900	2000	440
1956	299,792,700	2000	240
1956	299,791,900	2000	-560
1956	299,792,400	110	-60
1956	299,792,200	130	-260
1957	299,792,600	1200	140
1958	299,792,500	100	40
1960	299,792,600	60	140
1966	299,792,440	200	-20
1967	299,792,560	110	100
1967	299,792,500	50	40
1972	299,792,462	18	3?
1972	299,792,460	6	1?
1973	299,792,457.4	1.1	-1?
1973	299,792,458	2	?
1974	299,792,459	0.8	?
1978	299,792,458.8	0.2	?
1979	299,792,458.1	1.9	?
1983	299,792,458.6	0.3	?

It will be easy for us to understand how naturally scientists can fall into this trap and how the correcting process works; all

---

[15]The Atomic Constants, Light, and Time, by Trevor Norman and Barry Setterfield, C. 1987, Stanford Research Institute International, 333 Ravenswood Ave. Menlo Park, Ca. 94025, p. 26. "Real error" has been added here for comparison; it is the difference between each measurement and Light's actual speed — about 299,792,458 meters per second.

we need to do is to pretend for a moment that we are scientists who are trying to measure the speed of light:

First we read that another scientist has measured the speed of light and found it to be 300,400,000 m/s (meters per second). We try it ourselves and get 299,700,000 m/s. We were close but we wonder why we weren't closer. So we try again – still using the same equipment; this time we get 299,900,000 m/s. This looks "better" to us though in fact it is slightly less accurate. We make many more measurements "improving" our technique each time; but we rate our success largely on how close we come to 300,400,000 m/s; we have no other criteria to go by. Finally, we have "perfected" our technique and we are consistently measuring about 299,900,000 m/s; so we report our results.

We are almost certainly proud of our own ability and are quite willing to claim that the reason why our measurement differs from the earlier one is that ours is more accurate; but notice that we have still allowed it to influence our result slightly.

Eventually, better equipment comes along and the experiment is repeated with less error; but the scientists who repeat the experiment are also inclined to read the remaining error in favor of the traditional measurements. Each scientist in the chain is inclined to interpret the error in his instruments in favor of what the rest of the scientific community has found to be true before him. As time continues and instruments improve, scientists are forced farther away from the first mistake and converge upon the actual fact.

Like everyone, Norman and Setterfield certainly had their own expectations. As young-earth creationists, they presumably expected to discover that light used to travel faster in the past than it does now – enough so that light from the most distant stars could reach the earth within thousands of years. As they examined historic measurements of the speed of light, what they "saw" was that light has been slowing down ever since people started measuring it. Nearly all other scientists, in keeping with their expectations, "see" that the oldest measurements happened to be off and that subsequent measurements gradually corrected the measured speed down to the true value.

Norman and Setterfield selected a mathematical curve which not only fit the historic data reasonably well but which also indicated that light from the most distant stars took something on the order of six thousand years to reach us. A simple parabola, would have fit the data as well or better; but it would not have borne out their expectation that the speed of light was many millions of times greater six thousand years ago.[16]

When a scientist publishes his measurements, he usually reports an estimate of how much error they are likely to contain. Interestingly, the Norman-Setterfield curve conforms as well to this probable error as it does to the data points themselves. Most of the data points, which their curve follows, stray from the presently accepted value for light speed by about the amount of the predicted probable error. *This supports the hypothesis that the apparent change in light speed results from the reduction of measuring error with time.* It also tends to confirm the suspicion that scientists sometimes interpret their data to agree with what they believe to be true.

Norman and Setterfield also claim that the rate of radioactive decay must change as the speed of light changes.[17] They predict radiocarbon dates for 4000 year old wood will appear much older – by about 34 million years. As will be shown in the next chapter, carbon-14 dates for 4000-year-old wood turn out to be about 500 years *too young*. This observed <u>fact</u> refutes the Norman-Setterfield <u>theory</u> of light speed decay.

Although the Norman-Setterfield theory fails to stand up to close inspection, this does not prove that light from distant stars *couldn't* have reached us in mere thousands of years. Light still might have changed speed sometime in the past, even if there is no modern or historic data which confirms it. Light might have changed speed even if radioactive dating evidence doesn't confirm it. The real adversary of changing light speed – Einstein's theory of relativity – will be addressed next.

---

[16]Ibid p. 46. A parabola only triples light's speed for 6000 years ago. See <u>Geological Time and Scriptural Chronology</u>, Barry Setterfield, Box 318, Blackwood, S.A., 5051 Australia, p. 7, for the selected result.

[17]<u>The Atomic Constants, Light, and Time</u>, by Trevor Norman and Barry Setterfield, C. 1987, Stanford Research Institute International, 333 Ravenswood Ave. Menlo Park, Ca. 94025 p. 83.

Einstein's Theory of Relativity

Although popularly called the "theory" of relativity, Einstein's explanation has been experimentally tested for many years and has always done a good job of predicting the results of experiments. This gives relativity the status of scientific "law."[18]

In order to understand what relativity has to say about changing light speed, we need to know a little bit about relativity itself. This information will be presented as simply as possible. Although the following discourse is something of a brain exercise, most readers will probably find it quite interesting. The ideas behind relativity are not really very complicated; they are just very strange.

According to relativity, there is no preferred frame of reference. In other words, there is no place we can be, nor any speed at which we can be moving, that is more "true" in any sense than any other place or speed would be. In particular, it is impossible to ever know if we are moving very rapidly or are completely stopped. The laws of physics work just as well for a man in a high speed train as they do for one who is standing still. If the man in the train throws a ball straight up, it will come back down into his hand instead of hitting the back wall of the car in which he is riding. This is still true even if the man in the train thinks he is standing still. After all, the earth is a giant moving "spaceship" which is traveling very rapidly around the sun, yet all of the laws of physics work for us as we move, even though we regard ourselves as being stationary.

The moving train example is an over-simplified one. It is easily explained, even without relativity. Not all things can be explained without it, however. This is why the laws of relativity were needed. How Albert Einstein came to the conclusion that there is no preferred frame of reference is not only an interesting story, it may also help us understand what relativity is about.

It all started back in the last century with the Nobel-prize-winning scientist A.A. Michelson. Michelson had invented a

---

[18]This is true for the special theory at least. It is anticipated that the general theory of relativity will eventually need modification to harmonize it with quantum mechanics.

new measuring apparatus with which he hoped to accurately measure the velocity of "spaceship Earth." This attempt is known as the Michelson-Morley experiment.

It was known that the earth makes one revolution on its axis daily. Because the earth is nearly eight thousand miles in diameter, this means that a man standing at the equator is being carried along by the turning earth at a speed slightly over one thousand miles per hour.[19] Furthermore, the earth goes around the sun (total circular distance about 584,000,000 miles) once in a year. This means that the earth is zipping around the sun at more than 66,500 miles per hour. (And you are riding on it!) But how fast might the sun be moving through the galaxy or the galaxy through the universe? This is what Michelson wanted to measure.

Loosely speaking, Michelson's apparatus measured the speed of light as it passed the earth in one direction and very accurately compared it to the speed of light passing the earth in another direction. Because the earth was moving, it seemed to him that light should pass it at different speeds in different directions. As we have just seen, the earth is traveling at a pretty fast clip. The amazing result of the experiment was that no matter which way Michelson turned his apparatus, nor how carefully he made his measurement, he found that the apparent speed of passing light was always *exactly* the same – not *almost* the same; there was no observable difference at all!

Putting this into a common setting will reveal how absurd this measurement was. It was as if we were in a slowly moving car and we were watching faster cars on the same street which were passing us in both directions. Further, assume that all of those other cars were traveling at exactly the same speed, just like light does. We should expect cars which were overtaking us to pass us more slowly than those which where coming the opposite direction. What Michelson discovered was like saying that the cars were passing us at exactly the same rate in both

---

[19]He must travel 3.1416 (pi) times 7927 miles (the Earth's equatorial diameter) in 24 hours (how long it takes for the Earth to turn a complete circle) – which works out to be about 1037.6 mph (this ignores the correction for sidereal motion).

directions;[20] it was as if we were completely stopped. This was not at all what Michelson was expecting to discover! He knew that the earth was moving. Occasionally scientists discover things which they are not expecting – but only when the evidence demands it.

The scientific community had as hard a time accepting this as you might now be having. Michelson was given lots of money to reconstruct his apparatus and he rebuilt it using the best available techniques and equipment. This time his apparatus was built as solidly as a battleship. The experiment was repeated and, to the chagrin of the world, the results were exactly the same. The earth did not appear to be moving at all! Either the earth was the stationary center of the universe and the sun circled it, or new laws of physics were needed. Albert Einstein was able to figure out what had happened with Michelson's experiment; he provided the necessary new laws of physics to explain it.

Scientists found themselves in a position very much like the man on the train who could not tell from throwing his ball up into the air that he was moving – only their position was even worse; it was as if looking out the window wouldn't help either. According to the laws of relativity, the speed of light was what was always constant no matter how it was measured,[21] and other things like the very rate of *time* itself would change instead. When Einstein supplied this realization and the proper equations, Michelson's experiment made sense.

Apparently the rate of time actually does change! As it turns out, speed, acceleration and gravity all affect it.[22] As incredible as this sounds, subsequent experiments confirmed Einstein's seemingly wild claim. Elapsed time for very high speed particles can be shown to be quite different than that for a stationary observer.[23] Small effects can even be detected using very

---

[20]Because light had to make a round trip in Michelson's apparatus, he actually had to measure light traveling in two perpendicular directions. This makes the math more complex but the final result is exactly the same.

[21]Einstein's Universe, Nigel Calder, C. 1979, The Viking Press, N.Y., p. 105.

[22]Relativity, Albert Einstein Ph.D., C. 1931, Crown Publishers, N.Y., pp. 44, 117, (acceleration and gravity being equivalent, p. 83).

[23]The Feynman Lectures on Physics, Richard P. Feynman, C. 1983, Addison-Wesley Publishing Co., Reading, Massachusetts, p. 15-7.

accurate clocks carried on supersonic aircraft.[24] What time it is depends partly on where you are and how fast you are moving!

If one of a pair of identical twins were to be sent off into space for fifty years, traveling at speeds approaching the speed of light, something very strange would become apparent when both were reunited at the end of the journey. The earthbound twin would, naturally, find himself to be fifty years older than he had been; but the space traveler would have aged much less.[25] He could have aged as little as a year or less during his travels – depending on how fast he had been going. His spaceship was simply in something like what a science fiction writer might call a different "time warp." That's the way the real universe is; time passes at different rates under different conditions.

As previously mentioned, Norman and Setterfield's theory requires that the speed of light changes at the same rate everywhere in the universe; so it is always the same everywhere at any given instant. The problem with this is that ideas like "at the same time" lose meaning when time advances at different rates under different conditions. There is just no way to know whose clock to use.

In fact, it turns out that there is no way at all to synchronize two widely separated clocks so that everyone will agree that they are in fact synchronized. "Now" here is not necessarily also "now" in another place.[26] Two clocks which are close together (like on the same planet) can be synchronized fairly well, but as they are moved farther apart the situation becomes hopeless. If clock "A" were placed on earth and clock "B" somewhere in the M31 galaxy, the attempt to synchronize would be futile. Some observers would see clock "A" rust into powder before a shiny new clock "B" was even placed into position. Others would see

---

[24]"Around the World Atomic Clocks: Observed Relativistic Time Gains," J.C. Hafele and Richard E. Keating, SCIENCE, July 14, 1972, Vol. 177, No. 4044, pp. 168-170. See also "Around the World Atomic Clocks: Predicted Relativistic Time Gains," J.C. Hafele and Richard E. Keating, SCIENCE, July 14, 1972, Vol. 177, No. 4044, pp. 166-168.

[25]Einstein's Universe, Nigel Calder, C. 1979, The Viking Press, N.Y., p. 88.

[26]The Meaning Of Relativity, Albert Einstein, C. 1945, 1950, Princeton University Press, Princeton, pp. 30, 31. See also The Feynman Lectures on Physics, by Richard P. Feynman, C. 1963, Addison-Wesley Publishing Co., Reading, Mass., Vol. 1, p. 15-7.

"B" turn to powder before a shiny new "A" was positioned. This confusion would still be there even after corrections were made for the time it took the light to reach the different observers.[27]

God's View of Time

Now to put this all together: It is known from measurements that the speed of light, in empty space, is the same everywhere right now. It is also known from relativity that our "now" is the same as "then" for some other observer. This means the speed of light, for some other observer, must also have been the same everywhere "then." It follows that the speed of light, again in empty space, must always be the same everywhere, and for all time, because a chain of "thens" and "nows" can be linked together from different frames of reference to tie all time together. This is also true of other universal truths, besides the speed of light, for exactly the same reason. *Only those things which are able to have different values to different observers are able to change with time.*

In fact, according to Einstein's equations, time stands still for light in transit.[28] While billions of years might be passing for observers on planets, a photon[29] of light will make its flight from a distant star in a literal instant of its own time. It is as if light, like God, is not subject to what men call time. A traveling photon, if it could speak, might say with Jesus, "Before Abraham was born, I am!" (John 8:58).

All of this may sound like nonsense to many readers, but this *is* the way the universe is made. No promise was made that the universe would be easy to understand, only that it would speak the truth. Remember, it's like its Creator; He is not easy to fathom either! God made the universe with a very complex relationship to time. The universe speaks of *His* invisible

---

[27]Appendix 3 illustrates this problem of clock synchronization. It examines an interesting paradox which would result if time passed the way we normally supposed it to.

[28]Modern Physics: an Introductory Survey, by Arthur Beiser, C. 1968, Addison-Wesley Publishing Company, Reading, Mass., p. 38. In equation 2-29: $t=t_0/\sqrt{(1-v^2/c^2)}$; if $v=c$ then $t_0=0$ even if t is billions of years.

[29]A photon is the smallest possible "particle" of light.

attributes, not ours. To Him, a thousand years *really* is as one day and vice versa (2 Pet. 3:8). To us, a thousand years is a long, long time. As we study God's creation we should expect to see many more similarities between creation and Creator.

God uses His creation in many ways to teach us about Himself. He often teaches us spiritual truth through metaphors which, although they are mere shadows of spiritual truth, have been chosen from nature so carefully that their **physical** characteristics reflect in great detail the **spiritual** truths to which they relate.[30] For example, God sometimes calls us "sheep." We find that we can learn more about ourselves than we even care to know by studying real sheep in detail. In the words of a modern-day shepherd:

> "It is no mere whim on God's part to call us sheep. Our behavior patterns and life habits are so much like that of sheep it is well nigh embarrassing."
>
> A Shepherd Looks at Psalm 23, C. 1970, W. Phillip Keller, Zondervan, G.R., Mich., p. 74

Now that we understand that light's speed does not change,[31] we are in a better position to appreciate God's use of "light" as a metaphor. Truth and righteousness do not change from century to century but are forever the same. It appears that Jesus, who is the same yesterday, today and forever (Hebrews 13:8), and who could even say, "Before Abraham was born, I am!" (John 8:58), was speaking more graphically than many realize when He called Himself the "light" of the world (John 8:12).

Light cannot have changed speed at any time in the past. The very nature of God and His creation prohibit it.

---

[30]Or, possibly, the physical realities may have been created with the desired spiritual reflection in mind.

[31]As explained, this is true in free space only – light changes speed when it travels through a medium with a different index of refraction than empty space and also when it passes through a gravitational field. The physical world is, at best, a mere shadow of the spiritual reality.

Explanation #3
That light was created in transit

According to this explanation, light was created in transit between the distant stars and us. The light we see in the night sky was created to give the appearance of those stars but did not actually ever come from them. Those stars themselves do not really even need to be there at all. Indeed, according to this explanation, it is believed that exploding stars, such as the supernova observed on February 23, 1987, never existed! This particular supernova was 160,000 light-years away from us;[32] even the light from the flash which testified of the star's final death would necessarily have been created in transit. Any real light which this star's remains might have shed during the last ten thousand years would still remain in transit for the next 150,000 years.

In support of this "false appearance of age" theory, its proponents sometimes point to the creation of Adam as an example of God's methodology. They presume Adam was created with a built-in appearance of age, perhaps twenty or thirty years; but the Bible does not provide any specifics as to whether or not this is true. Because it is merely presumed to be true, it is useless as supporting evidence. Adam might have been created as a baby or even as an embryo. The embryo possibility has some fascinating scriptural support; although it would be an unnecessary and lengthy digression to examine it here, this theory may be presented in a later book.

This explanation is also part of a more general theory about all scientific data indicating antiquity; according to the general theory, God created the universe as it presently appears, with all of the evidence consistent with an old age built right into it.[33] Dinosaur bones (which are found in sediments dating much older

---

[32]"The Great Supernova of 1987," by Stan Woosley and Tom Weaver, SCIENTIFIC AMERICAN, August 1989, Vol. 261, No. 2, p. 32.

[33]This young-earth position is different from the one which claims that the actual scientific evidence refutes the old-earth position. These two young-earth positions are in disagreement with each other over the validity of the universe's evidence.

than ten thousand years) would have been fabricated by God and planted to give the false appearance of an old earth. This would mean that they were never really part of living animals but only hints at many very interesting kinds of animals which never really existed. Also, the radioactive isotopes, which are used to date these fossils, would have been strategically planted at various levels of geological formations to give the false appearance of different ages depending on their location.

According to explanation #3, starlight speaks of an old earth but it speaks falsely. It is difficult to refute this hypothesis scientifically; all evidence would lie. Similarly, it would be difficult to prove scientifically that the universe (including our memories of it) was not just created yesterday! If we were to take this position we would have no trouble at all sidestepping any scientific evidence; but we would still have considerable difficulty with the Biblical evidence.

To begin with, the thought of God fabricating and hiding dinosaur bones is strongly reminiscent of Piltdown man.[34] In 1912 a human skull was "discovered" near Piltdown, England which was accompanied by a fragment of an orangutan's jaw. The jaw had been filed to imitate human tooth wear. Both it and the skull had been stained to give the appearance of age. They had been buried together with some genuine ancient animal fossils – apparently as a prank. This prank got out of hand when its suspected prime perpetrator died. Any possible accomplices were, presumably, too embarrassed to confess; so the "fossil" was largely accepted by the scientific community as an ancient ancestor of man. It was not discovered to be a fraud until 1953. By then, sadly, much scientific effort had been wasted and many men had been made to appear very foolish.

This is not the sort of thing we should suspect God of doing. It's too much like telling a lie; and God doesn't lie. The previous chapter dealt with the way in which God sometimes *hides* truth from people to keep them from having any particular advantage over others. God does not always reveal Himself in the plainest possible way; but the line must be drawn here. Explanation #3

---

[34]Hen's Teeth and Horse's Toes, by Stephen Jay Gould, C. 1983, W.W. Norton and Company, N.Y., pp. 201-226. See for more detail concerning Piltdown man.

has God fabricating false evidence. This is not the same as speaking the truth in parables or cryptic language. There is no way to explain fabricated dinosaur bones or flashes from nonexistent exploding stars as camouflaged truth. Under explanation #3, their existence would have to be an outright deception. It simply cannot be allowed that God would bear this kind of false witness.[35] It would seem that those who have suggested this explanation have not fully thought out its consequences.

Whether the general form of this explanation is assumed, or nothing but starlight is taken to have been created with a false appearance of age, it is still a deception. If we had never really seen the depths of the heavens but only a contrived image of them, God would *not* be telling us that they declare His glory (Psalm 19:1). It is certain that "liar" is not one of God's invisible attributes. It is therefore certain that nowhere can "liar" be seen or understood from the things which have been made in the way that Paul assures us that God's invisible attributes can be (Romans 1:20). God's very nature eliminates explanation #3 as a possibility – especially when His nature is considered in conjunction with the fact that we can read His invisible attributes in His creation.

A non-literal meaning should never be forced on the heavens if the literal reading makes sense. The same rules which help us interpret God's Bible must apply to His creation as well. This is especially true if the non-literal interpretation carries the consequence that God bears a false witness in His creation.

If God's Bible had said "the universe is young" as clearly as His universe testifies it is old, then we might have to appeal to a deceptively non-literal reading of either God's Bible or His creation. We would either have to assume that God created light between the heavens and our eyes or between our Bibles and our eyes. Either way the truth is assumed to be something different than what our own eyes report to us. Fortunately, this is *not* our

---

[35]Even in 2 Thessalonians 2:11 where it says, "God sends them a powerful delusion so that they will believe the lie," God does not directly send this delusion Himself. As explained in 2 Thess. 2:7-11, the delusion is brought by Satan; God merely stops holding him back. As Psalms 19:1 and Romans 1:20 attest, we see God's handiwork, not Satan's, when we study the creation.

position! God has not given us any such contradiction. Both God's Bible and His creation mean *exactly* what they say; we only have to be careful and keep our eyes open when we read them.

Even if we were willing to allow this sort of deception on God's part, Einstein's Theory of relativity will, once again, give us trouble. The problem is that the "false appearance of age" theory demands that the entire universe be created nearly "simultaneously."[36] As we have seen, the word "simultaneously" has no absolute meaning in God's universe. His time is not our time. Even in our narrow earthly frame of reference, we are still going to need billions of years of real antiquity somewhere. The problem is that "clocks" on distant quasars are marking time so slowly[37] that they have lagged billions of years into the past (as measured from the big bang, when all matter was in one place and the universe had only one frame of reference). Even under the "false appearance of age" theory, these objects exist in the *very* distant past when viewed from our own present frame of reference,.

The old-earth position is consistent with both the physical and Biblical evidence. That it is consistent with the scientific evidence, will be demonstrated in Chapters 5 and 6. Chapter 6 will also demonstrate that the old-earth position can be reconciled with every single word in the first chapter of Genesis.

Conclusions

All three of the suggested explanations have failed; the stars are certainly very far away from us, light has always traveled at the same speed, and God does not lie to us in His creation. There is no way light from the most distant stars could be seen from earth if the universe were very young. There are simply no other reasonable possibilities.

---

[36]In cosmological terms, six consecutive twenty-four-hour days comprise a mere instant.

[37]This follows from relativity because quasars are moving away from us very rapidly.

What this leaves is a universe which is certainly very old. There seems to be no way to compromise with the ten-thousand-year age proposed by the young-earth creationists. At least one of the "days" of Genesis must have been greatly longer than twenty-four hours. Because the young-earth creationists simply cannot be correct about this, and because the scientists have good reasons for suggesting the dates which they propose, the best course of action is to accept the scientific dates as being approximately correct.

Chapter 5:
The Testimony of Many Witnesses

"Every matter must be established by the testimony of two or three witnesses."

−2 Corinthians 13:1.

If the Bible does not require that the universe is young, and if God's universe itself testifies that it is old, then the question should be settled; the "days" of Genesis 1 were very long periods of time. Still, it is likely that more proof will be needed to convince some readers. This is because many Christians have a false picture of scientific knowledge − one in which the universe's facts are no more than a confused collection of contradictions, and hence, cannot be trusted. Consider, for example, the following quotation by a young-earth creationist:

"... the creation model permits us to look seriously at those natural processes which seem to favor a young earth and a recent creation. We shall see later in this chapter that there exist many such processes. Unfortunately most people do not know this, since we were all indoctrinated as children in school, with one model of origins exclusively. Only those processes which seem to favor an exceedingly old earth and old universe were included in our instruction."[1]

---

[1]Scientific Creationism, Ed. by Henry M. Morris Ph.D., C. 1974, Master Books, El Cajon, Ca., pp. 136, 137.

Here the claim is made that the evidence sometimes points to a young universe and sometimes to an old one. Is this possible? The physical universe is the work of God. Like His Bible, God's universe will always tell us the truth. Such a witness can never contradict itself because truth is not like that. It follows that once the universe has testified that it is either young or old, it should always do the same.

Even if the universe itself is always truthful, those who report its facts to us will not necessarily understand them correctly. Because young-earth creationists disagree with other scientists about what the data says, it follows that someone must be making mistakes. Under these circumstances we need to be careful about what we decide to believe. There will be some errors presented to us just as though they were the universe's actual facts.

The Bible provides a method for how we are to deal with a similar situation; in Deuteronomy 19:15, we are told:

"One witness is not enough to convict a man accused of any crime or offense he may have committed. A matter must be established by the testimony of two or three witnesses."

One witness would have been enough if we could be sure that he would always tell the truth; but since a witness might lie, the law tells us that we need more. If two witnesses both know and tell the truth, their testimonies will always agree with each other; but two witnesses who lie will sometimes disagree; they have no real facts with which to guide themselves. (See Mark 14:55-59.) Of course even truthful witnesses will disagree with each other if they do not have a firm enough knowledge of the whole situation; but when this happens we cannot use their testimonies with confidence.

This chapter will examine the testimony of many "witnesses" concerning the age of God's creation. These "witnesses" will be the evidences from various scientific fields of study: tree rings, lake sediments, moon dust, volcanic action, erosion, and radioactive dating.

Tree Rings

Of the myriad different ways to tell how old different things are, one of the first ones we learn, often as children, is that we can tell how old a tree is by counting its annual rings. The tree does not even need to be cut down if a thin core is taken. This method is quite easy to understand.

When a tree grows, it adds wood to its outside layer just under the bark. Trees tend to do most of their growing in the spring and summer and to sit dormantly through the winter. This means that wood is added to the outside of the tree in spurts once a year. These growth spurts are easily visible as annual rings in the grain of the wood. Although a tree itself may be alive, the wood at its center is actually dead. The tree is alive only on its surface where the bark is. This is why a hollow tree can survive, but removing the bark from around a tree will kill it. Each year another ring is added to the dead core of wood. Interestingly, each of the rings in a tree will actually have a slightly different carbon-14 date.

As it happens, some trees live for very long periods of time; Bristlecone pine trees, which grow in the White Mountains of California, live for many thousands of years. One lived over 5000 years before it was, unfortunately, cut down in 1964.[2]

There is another thing, other than the age of a tree, which can be determined from studying tree rings. Scientists can determine how suitable the weather was for tree growing, each year of a tree's life. During good years, most of the trees in a particular forest will add wide growth rings – during poor years, thin growth rings. Because scientists can count years (rings) backwards from the present (just below the bark), they can figure, quite accurately, which years were good and which were poor for growing trees.

This effect can be used to extend the tree-ring sequence back additional thousands of years by using older dead wood which can be found on the ground. Ring patterns in the dead wood can be compared with those in living trees. Where clear evidence of

---

[2]"Dendrochronology and Serendipity," by Charles J. Hitch, AMERICAN SCIENTIST, May-June 1982, Vol. 70, No. 3, pp. 302-303.

overlap occurs, the ring sequence of the older dead tree can be added to the living one. Overlap can be seen since the growth patterns will be the same for any trees within a local area whose lifetimes once overlapped. This is because the weather during those years (and hence the relative widths of the related rings) would have been the same for all of those trees. By this method, the tree ring chronology for Bristlecone pines has been extended back about 9000 years as of 1982.[3]

Now 9000 years is not the age of the universe nor even that of the earth. This is a minimum age for one single group of trees in California. Obviously, the soil and rocks which lie under those trees were laid down earlier still. This example was chosen as a first step because it is easy to understand (no nuclear physics involved) and because it demonstrates basic principles which will be used in some of the following examples.

Annual Layers in Sediments

Trees are not the only things in God's creation which keep a yearly record of time; sediments which accumulate in the bottoms of lakes do this too. Different seasons create different conditions for a lake which are reflected in different types of sediment layers. In spring and summer, the layer is rich in calcium carbonate (limestone which dissolves in water). Sediments from the rest of the year are rich in organic material. These layers, which are called "varves," pile up year after year and keep a record of the annual cycles. The Green River Formation, of Utah, Colorado and Wyoming, contains a record which is more than four million annual layers deep.[4] Obviously, this means that the lake bottom which accumulated those alternating layers of sediment existed for millions of years. Even this is not the age of the earth; it is only the length of time one particular lake existed.

Like the previous example, this process of layer formation is easy to understand and the record of elapsed time is easy to read.

---

[3]Ibid p. 302.

[4]Pages of Stone, Halka Chronic, C. 1984, The Mountaineers, 306 2nd Avenue West, Seattle, Washington 98119, pp. 70-74.

There is no easy way to misunderstand the evidence. This evidence, and the evidence of starlight from the previous chapter, establishes that the universe must be millions of years old at the very least.[5]

Moon Dust

Young-earth creationists argue that scientists only concentrate on those methods of dating which yield old ages, arbitrarily ignoring any method which does not give an old enough age. One young-earth argument involves moon dust. Because this argument is often cited, it will be examined in some detail.

The amount of dust on the surface of the moon is presented as if it were evidence that the universe is young. According to this argument, it has been estimated that a large quantity of meteoric dust falls onto the earth each year; assuming that the rate of dust falling onto the moon is about the same as that estimated for the earth, it would seem that there should be a great deal of dust piled up on the moon. It is argued that there is insufficient dust on the moon's surface if the moon is billions of years old.

Unlike the moon, the earth is an active environment. Therefore, the dust which settles onto it does not form an undisturbed layer. What has happened to this dust on the earth will be briefly considered at the end of this chapter. Arguments from two different young-earth sources which concern the moon's dust will be examined here:

Source #1

"Hans Pettersson of the Swedish Oceanographic Institute calculated that about 14.3 million tons of meteoritic dust of the type which contain nickel settles to earth each year. Isaac Asimov has calculated that, if this rate has continued unaltered for the past 5 billion years, then there should be

---

[5]Other evidence, such as light from astronomical objects more distant than M31, establishes that the universe is actually billions of years old.

a layer of meteoric dust at least 54 feet thick all over the earth. No such layer is found." [p. 162]

"Prior to our first manned moon landing, some NASA scientists predicted that there might be as much as 54 feet of this lunar soil, assuming the age of the moon to be about 5 billion years and assuming that meteorites had been falling on the moon at the present rate since or near the beginning of its birth. We now know that no such thick surface layer exists. Instead, the most recent estimates of average regolith thickness are as follows:

"(a) Near the Apollo 11 site, in the Sea of Tranquility, 13 feet.

"(b) Near the Apollo 12 site, in the Ocean of Storms, 11 1/2 feet.

"(c) Near the Luna 16 site, in the Sea of Fertility, 2-3 feet. (According to theory, Fertility soil should have been thicker than the other since it is an 'older' area.)

"It appears that this 'timer,' the build-up of moon soil, has not been 'running' for about 5 billion years, but rather, has only recently been 'turned on.'" [pp. 150-151.]

Science and Creation, by William W. Boardman Jr. et al., C. 1973, Creation-Science Research Center, San Diego, Ca., pp. 162, 150-151.

Source #2

"It is known that there is essentially a constant rate of cosmic dust particles entering the earth's atmosphere from space and then gradually settling to the earth's surface. The best measurements of this influx have been made by Hans Pettersson, who obtained the figure of 14 million tons per year. This amounts to 14×10^{19} pounds in 5 billion years. If we assume the density of compacted dust is, say, 140 pounds per cubic foot, this corresponds to a volume of 10^{18} cubic feet. Since the earth has a surface area of approximately 5.5×10^{15} square feet, this seems to mean that there should have accumulated during the 5-billion-year age of the earth, a layer of meteoric dust approximately 182 feet thick all over the world!

"There is not the slightest sign of such a dust layer anywhere of course. On the moon's surface it should be at least as thick, but the astronauts found no sign of it (before the moon landings, there was considerable fear that the men would sink into the dust when they arrived on the moon, but no comment has apparently ever been made by the authorities as to why it wasn't there as anticipated)."

Scientific Creationism, Ed. by Henry M. Morris Ph.D., C. 1974, Master Books, El Cajon, Ca., pp. 151, 152.

In summary, what is claimed concerning moon dust (which is also called lunar soil or regolith) is as follows:

Moon Dust Claims:

1) That according to Hans Pettersson's earth-based measurements of meteoric influx there should be at least 54 feet of dust on the surface of the earth – or at least 182 feet depending upon whose estimate we use. A similar layer should be on the surface of the moon.
2) That the dust layer on the moon's surface should be at least as thick as a hypothetical layer calculated for the earth using earth's meteoric influx data.
3) That the depth of this dust is: 13 feet near the Apollo 11 site, in the Sea of Tranquility; 11 1/2 feet near the Apollo 12 site, in the Ocean of Storms; and 2-3 feet near the Luna 16 site, in the Sea of Fertility.
4) That according to theory, the soil at the Sea of Fertility should have been thicker than the other areas since it is an "older" area.
5) That the astronauts found no sign of this heavy dust layer and that authorities have not commented as to why it wasn't there as anticipated.

Difficulties emerge as we compare these various claims with other information, including NASA's testimony about the Apollo flights.

Claim #1

That earth-based measurements predict a great deal of dust on the moon.

This claim says that dust is falling onto the earth at a rate which would have resulted in a very deep pile if it were left undisturbed over billions of years (no rain washing it away – no volcanos burying it, etc.). Because the surface of the moon has been left virtually undisturbed – there is no weather there – this dust should be visible if the universe is very old.

The problem is the data used to calculate the 54-foot or 182-foot depths is out of date. Recent measurements tell us that this influx to the earth is actually 1000 times less than Pettersson originally estimated way back in 1960.[6] Clearly this first claim is an error. It is based on very obsolete data.

Claim #2

That the dust on the moon's surface should be at least as thick as that estimated from the earth's data.

Because this second claim is based on the same faulty data as the first claim was, we should expect it to be in error as well. Many different determinations of the influx to the moon's surface have been made which confirm this.[7] Direct measurements were even made on the moon by the Apollo astronauts using collector targets.[8] Very little meteoric dust actually falls onto the moon.

---

[6]The Cambridge Encyclopedia of Earth Sciences, Ed. Davis G. Smith Ph.D., C. 1981, Crown Publishers Inc. / Cambridge University Press, N.Y., p. 33.

[7]The Soviet-American Conference on Cosmochemistry of the Moon and Planets, 1977, NASA SP-370, (Vol. 2) , pp. 659, 664.

[8]For example, pieces of the Surveyor III spacecraft were recovered by a later flight and examined for micrometeorites. Ibid p. 595.

The next two claims (3 and 4) will be taken in reverse order to simplify things.

Claim #4

That, according to theory, the soil at the Sea of Fertility should have been thicker than soil at the other areas since it is an "older" area.

This fourth claim, gets progressively weaker the closer it is traced to its source. The publication which the authors of Science and Creation are quoting is the January 23, 1971 issue of SCIENCE NEWS where three soil depths (of claim #3 below) are given in a brief news item with a comment on the fact that the Luna 16 core presented some surprises. From this 35 centimeter (14 inch) core the Soviet scientist Vinogradov concluded that the depth of the dust was "possibly 0.5 to 1 meter."[9] Notice his use here of the word "possibly." This puts the evidence in a less definite light.

Three pages earlier in the same issue of SCIENCE NEWS, we see how Vinogradov arrived at this conclusion. "The Luna 16 drill hit a solid object (which he says could have been bedrock)."[10] It is also possible that the solid object was nothing more than a large buried rock. Luna 16 was unmanned and so it only had one chance to take its sample; it had no way to walk over a few feet and try again.

Although it is claimed that Fertility soil should have been thicker than soil from the other areas, since it is an "older" area, it is not clear that Fertility soil isn't deeper. As this fact has been traced back toward its source, it looks less like proof that the scientists were wrong about moon dust, and more like one Soviet probe may have had the bad luck of hitting a rock after drilling only about 14 inches.

---

[9] "Lunar Sciences: Luna 16, An Unusual Core," SCIENCE NEWS, January 23, 1971, Vol. 99, No. 4, p. 65.

[10] "At the Moon Conference: Consensus and Conflict," SCIENCE NEWS, January 23, 1971, Vol. 99, No. 4, p. 62.

Claim #3

That the dust on the moon at three locations was 13, 11.5 and 2-3 feet deep.

The Luna 16 data point (the 2-3 foot deep one) has already been examined. It is not specifically stated in SCIENCE NEWS whether the Apollo 11 and 12 cores (the other two locations mentioned here) actually bottomed out against bedrock or whether the numbers given were just the length of the cores taken and, hence, would only indicate a minimum depth. In any case, more recent Apollo flights tell us much more.

By the time of the Apollo 16 flight, some more sophisticated experiments had been performed. In NASA's preliminary report on the Apollo 16 mission, results of a seismic experiment are given which place the depth of the lunar soil at about 12.2 meters (40 feet).[11]

This large depth could not easily have been determined by merely driving a core rod through it. The astronauts had great difficulty driving even a 10 foot core into the moon's soil;[12] in the moon's low gravity it was hard for the astronauts to press downward, and the moon dust presented an unexpected amount of resistance. The lunar soil is not exposed to weathering effects so the individual grains are jagged and catch on each other. Footprints sink into it even less than they would into sand on a beach. This is why the astronaut's footprints were so shallow.

Finally, there is a NASA report titled, The Soviet-American Conference on Cosmochemistry of the Moon and Planets.[13] This report is a source which, in this author's opinion, contains everything anyone ever wanted to know about meteoric influx and the depth of moon dust. As this report explains on page 574, the moon's "maria" (the darker, more recently melted areas) have dust piled several meters thick over them; but that its

---

[11] Apollo 16, Preliminary Report, 1972, NASA SP-315, pp. 10-1, 10-2.

[12] New Worlds For Old, Duncan Lunan, C. 1979, William Morrow and Company, Inc., N.Y., p. 81.

[13] The Soviet-American Conference on Cosmochemistry of the Moon and Planets, 1977, NASA SP-370, (Vol. 2), pp. 571-664. This very technical source was not selected for ease of understanding but to demonstrate just how much work NASA has put into studying the moon's dust.

"continental regions" are piled as deeply as dozens of meters thick[14] – this would be about 100 feet.

Also in this same NASA report, the effect of the falling meteoric dust on the soil is shown in terms of the amount of mixing of the soil over various time spans. The falling dust, at present-day rates, is so low that it would have taken a billion years to have even stirred up the moon's top 10 centimeters (4 inches).[15] As it turns out, this rate has not been constant over the moon's lifetime; it will be seen in the next chapter why the amount of falling dust would have been much greater in the early days while the solar system (the earth, sun, moon and planets) was still being formed. This is because of the way God created our solar system.

Claim #5

That astronauts found no sign of this dust and that no comment has been made by the authorities as to why it wasn't there as anticipated.

This claim is clearly in error. A great deal of dust covers the moon; and NASA has released reams of information concerning it. This information is sufficient in scope and detail to bore a researcher to tears. Of course not *all* of this information was available back in 1973 and 1974 when these moon dust arguments were originally composed; but it is certainly available to us now.[16]

In conclusion, it is obvious that the amount of dust on the moon does *not* indicate a young earth. The testimonies of some young-earth creationists have been compared with the testimony of NASA and were found to disagree. Because everyone must get their information indirectly through NASA, the error must be in the young-earth testimonies. There is nowhere else, other than the moon landings, that they could obtain their information.

---

[14]Ibid p. 574.

[15]Ibid p. 625.

[16]The Apollo 16 information *was* available back in 1972.

Volcanos and Erosion

There are right and wrong ways to read the Bible. One wrong way is to take a single verse out of context and to simply ignore the rest of scripture. The only correct way to study the Bible is to examine *all* of the scriptural evidence. The same rule also applies to the study of God's creation. The following will compare the testimonies of two young-earth arguments to illustrate a failure to study God's creation in its full context. The first argument concerns how much mass is being added to the continents each year:

"... it seems reasonable to assume that at least 10 cubic kilometers of new igneous rocks are formed each year by flows from the earth's mantle.

"The total volume of the earth's crust is about $5x10^9$ cubic kilometers. Thus, the entire crust could have been formed by volcanic activity at present rates in only 500 million years, which would only take us back into the Cambrian period. On the other hand, all geologists would surely agree that practically all the earth's crust had been formed billions of years before that time. The uniformitarian model once again leads to a serious problem and contradiction."[17]

Because volcanic rock is being continuously added to the earth's crust and because only so much crust has piled up, we are expected to conclude that the earth must be young. This argument is quite easy to understand and sounds valid, but it represents a single scientific fact being removed from the context of other related scientific facts. What is worse, the critical scientific context from which this has been removed was presented only two pages earlier in the same book:

"Approximately 27.5 billion tons of sediment are being transported to the ocean every year. The total mass of sediments already in the ocean is about 820 million billion

---

[17]Scientific Creationism, Ed. by Henry M. Morris Ph.D., C. 1974, Master Books, El Cajon, Ca., p. 157.

tons. Dividing the total mass by the transport rate yields 30 million years as the maximum age of the ocean since sediments first started to flow into it ... the total mass of continental rocks above sea level is only about 383 million billion tons, ... Thus, in only 383/27.5, or 14, million years, the present continents, eroding at present rates, would have been eroded to sea level!"[18]

Here also, we are told that there is an upper limit to how old the earth can be. Otherwise, all of the dirt that exists would have washed down into the ocean by now. This argument would also look good if it were taken all by itself; but notice what happens to the two arguments when they are examined together – in the greater context which their combined information provides.

In the first argument, we are told that each year volcanic activity adds at least 10 cubic kilometers to the earth's crust; in the second, we are told that each year rivers are washing 27.5 billion tons of this away. These two work out to be the same amount – the two processes balance each other almost exactly.[19]

This material finally settles to the ocean floor, but it does not remain there forever. The sea floor is not stationary; it slides around, riding on the slowly moving plates of rock which make up the earth's surface. Sediments are ultimately carried back down into the hot interior parts of the earth.[20] Some of this material eventually gets recycled by volcanic activity; it completes the cycle by returning to the earth's crust – only to be washed away again.

So what has happened to the two arguments? Both have been shown to be worthless. Their supporting scientific evidence has

---

[18]Ibid p. 155.

[19]The average density of the continents is 2.67 g/cc. Therefore, 10 cubic kilometers of continental mass would weigh about 26.7 billion metric tons – or 29.4 billion short tons. See the Handbook of Chemistry and Physics 49th Edition, Ed. Robert C. Weast, Ph.D., C. 1964, The Chemical Rubber Company, Cleveland, Ohio, p. F-144.

[20]Continents in Collision, by Russell Miller, C. 1983, Time-Life Books, Alexandria, Virginia, pp. 80-82. The world's ocean floors are swept clean by plate motion every 300-400 million years.

simply been taken out of the context of the full testimony of the earth's evidence.

One might just as well have argued that the earth must be young because, "All streams flow into the sea, yet the sea is never full." (Ecc. 1:7); but as Solomon continues and explains: "To the place the streams come from, there they return again." (Also Ecc. 1:7). God designed the world in such a way that it can operate well for a long time. As Paul said, the creation was made to reflect the invisible attributes of its Creator (Romans 1:20) and He is *not about* to run down either.

Again, when witnesses for the young-earth position are examined, errors are found in their testimony. This author does not believe that the men who have presented these arguments are deliberately trying to misrepresent the facts; but it is inescapable that they have not been as careful in checking things out as they should have been.

Radioactive Dating

Another witness to the great age of the earth is the evidence from radioactive isotopes – radiation dating. It almost seems like no creationist's book is complete without a chapter devoted to pointing out its problems – often imaginary ones. In this book, radiation dating will be explained in enough detail that the reader may get a feel for himself of where problems exist and where they do not. Where the problems are not significant, radioactive dating becomes another of the universe's witnesses to the truth. Anything that can be used to help determine the truth is really on our side!

Different types of radioactive dating are useful for different situations and age ranges. Some types of uranium, for example, can be used to date very old things[21] (ages in billions of years such as the solar system). However, these are not very useful for more recent things (mere millions of years). The potassium-argon method is good for the millions-to-billions-of-years range;

---

[21]Because the uranium dating method is very involved, we will not go into it here. Determining the original quantities involves correlating many different isotope concentrations.

but it is only accurate to about the nearest fifty thousand years at best. Also, it can only be used on volcanic materials; one is not likely to find a handy lava flow in the vicinity of, and within 100,000 years of a fossil which one might be trying to date. For these reasons, it is generally not considered to be useful for dating specimens younger than about half a million years of age. Carbon-14 has a useful range that roughly spans the age of modern man. This makes it useful to archaeologists.

Carbon-14

Normal everyday carbon-12 has six protons and six neutrons.[22] Six plus six is twelve which is why it is called carbon-12. The electrons are not counted here. Carbon-14 has six protons (like carbon-12) but has eight neutrons – which totals fourteen. Carbon-12 is stable, which means that it lasts forever. Carbon-14 is not, which means that it changes into something else when given enough time. What happens to carbon-14 is that one of the extra neutrons will suddenly split apart into an electron (which will be ignored) and a proton (which won't). This means there will then be seven protons and seven neutrons. An atom having seven protons and seven neutrons is not carbon, but nitrogen (specifically nitrogen-14).

The rate at which carbon-14 turns into nitrogen-14 has been accurately measured in laboratories and has been found to be quite constant. Decay rates are constant under all conditions for which life is possible; altering those rates takes heroic effort. They can be altered by a small fraction of a percent with pressures so great that the very atoms themselves begin to crush (over one million pounds per square inch).[23] Although rates can be changed significantly by intense neutron radiation,[24] this

---

[22]Carbon (including both normal C-12 and radioactive C-14) is the stuff that coal, graphite (pencil "lead"), and diamonds are made of. It is also a major part of gasoline, limestone, sugar, fireplace ashes and of every living creature.

[23]"Pressure Dependence of the Radioactive Decay Constant of Beryllium-7," W.K. Hensley, et al, SCIENCE, Sept. 21, 1973, Vol. 181, No. 4105, p. 1164.

[24]This is how atom bombs work – U-235 which normally has a half-life of 700 million years is made to decay almost instantly in a chain reaction. Still, the only reasonable position concerning fossil artifacts is that the decay rates have been perfectly constant. There is simply no way that billions of years' worth of nuclear energy could have been quickly released within the earth in a few

generates different decay products than normally would be formed; this means there would be evidence if this happened.[25]

What has been found, based on laboratory measurements, is that after a period of about 5770 years, half of the atoms in a lump of pure carbon-14 will turn into nitrogen-14. This is called its "half-life." In another 5770 years, half of the remaining half will also turn into nitrogen-14 (*not all* of the remaining half) and so on. After three half-lives, only 1/8 of the original carbon-14 would remain. The nitrogen produced eventually escapes into the air, which is mostly nitrogen anyway.

Now, if it could be known how much carbon-14 there was in a particular sample at the beginning (for C-14 this corresponds to the time when a particular living thing died), the remaining amount could be used to figure out how long that sample had been around. If only one fourth of the original C-14 remained, then it would follow that the original amount had been reduced by half two times. This would mean that the sample had been sitting for 5770 + 5770 years or 11,540 years.

As with any useful radioactive dating method, it turns out there *is* a way to know how much of what was originally present. Otherwise the method would be unusable. How much carbon-14 was originally present in a plant or animal at the moment of its death can be determined from the amount of carbon-12 which is still present in that specimen. Here is how:

New carbon-14 is constantly being produced from nitrogen-14 by cosmic rays in the upper atmosphere at about the same rate at which the old carbon-14 is decaying back into nitrogen. The rate of production does change a little from year to year and from century to century; but the ratio between the number of

---

thousand years (at least a million times faster than normally) without there being evidence of that much extra released heat. According to The Cambridge Encyclopedia of Earth Sciences, Ed. David G. Smith, C. 1981, Crown Publishers Inc./Cambridge University Press, N.Y., p. 151, the earth's radioactive elements normally release 9.5×10^{20} Joules of heat per year – that's a lot of energy – 30 million megawatts continuously for 4.5 billion years)

[25]For example, argon-40 is produced by potassium which has been left sitting around for millions of years, but argon-39 is produced when the same sample is exposed to neutron radiation. "Argon-40/Argon-39 Dating of Lunar Rock Samples," by Grenville Turner, SCIENCE, January 30, 1970, Vol. 167, No. 3918, p. 466.

C-12 atoms and C-14 atoms in the air is, more-or-less, always constant. What variation there is will be considered later.

Newly-formed carbon-14 quickly reacts into carbon dioxide, which plants are continually taking in from the air and converting into oxygen and other things like sugar. This is how plants grow. They build themselves up from atoms, including the carbon which they get from the carbon dioxide in the air, and from other atoms which they get from soil and water. Similarly, animals eat the plants and therefore build themselves from the same atoms. Even animals which eat other animals (for example we ourselves) are eating carbon atoms which were recently taken from the air by plants which the food animal ate. This means that whatever C-12/C-14 ratio happens to be in the air at any given time is the same as the C-12/C-14 ratio which exists in all living plants and animals at that time.

When a plant or animal dies, it stops eating and breathing so it no longer exchanges its carbon with that in the air. This means that the C-14 slowly starts to disappear (by turning into nitrogen gas) while the C-12 stays put. Furthermore, because C-12 and C-14 are chemically identical, any chemical reaction which might remove the C-14 from a specimen will also remove the C-12 by the same fractional amount. This will have no effect on the calculated date.

In a laboratory, the amounts of C-12 and C-14 can be accurately measured. Because C-12 lasts forever, the amount of it in a fossil animal is the same as the amount it had when it died. Because it is approximately known how many C-14 atoms were originally present for every C-12 atom, it follows that the original amount of C-14 can be calculated. Thus everything is known which is needed to figure out how long ago the specimen died.

There are still some problems; one is that the sample can be contaminated by other material containing carbon with a different C-12/C-14 ratio. When we closely examine an old bone, we notice that it is full of little holes like a sponge. This means that it can soak things up. Teeth, tusks and antlers are also porous. This does not make the C-14 method unusable. It just means that scientists have to be a little more careful when they try to date this type of specimen. Limestone, which also contains carbon, will often soak into these holes during the thousands of years while a sample is buried. When this happens, it must be washed out before accurate dating can be done. Acid is used for this wash because limestone dissolves readily in acid while bones, teeth, tusks and antlers do not.

This acid wash was apparently misunderstood in one young-earth argument which claimed that, "Yale University dated an antler three different times and got three different ages – 5,340 years, 9,310 years, and 10,320 years."[26] We might picture in our minds a very confused scientist until we check the original source where we find that the three dates were: the antler when it was contaminated with recently formed limestone – 9,310 years, the antler after the limestone had been washed out – 10,320 years, and the limestone itself which had been washed out into the acid – 5,340 years.[27] And so, when we look more closely, this turns out to be a perfectly reasonable set of measurements.[28]

Another type of contamination occurs when an animal eats very old rotten vegetation instead of fresh. If a living mollusk – a general type of animal including aquatic (water-living) snails – eats only muck which has been dead for thousands of years, he will eventually carbon-14 date the same age as that muck. This is common for bottom-feeding snails which live in muddy rivers where very old sediments are constantly being churned up. According to C-14's theoretical basis, "You are what you eat;" for these snails, this can be vegetation which has been dead for 3000 years. This is not usually a problem because most animals are more careful about what they eat. Neither is this a problem for aquatic snails which live in clear lakes or in the ocean.[29]

---

[26]Reasons Skeptics Should Consider Christianity, by Josh McDowell and Don Stewart, C. 1981, Here's Life Publishers, P.O. Box 1576, San Bernardino, CA 92402, p. 116.

[27]"Yale Natural Radiocarbon Measurements," by G.W. Barendsen, SCIENCE, November 1, 1957, Vol. 126, No. 3279, p. 911. See sample Y-159, -1, -2, & the explanation for the preceding sample Y-158.

[28]Also, the accuracy of the C-14 method has been greatly improved since this **1957** measurement was made.

[29]"Radiocarbon Dating: Fictitious Results With Mollusk Shells," M.L. Keith and G.M. Anderson, SCIENCE, August 16, 1983, Vol. 141, No. 3581, pp. 634-636. 3000 years seems to represent a maximum limit for this problem in those few situations where it can occur at all.

One other problem is that scientists don't really know exactly how many C-14 per C-12 atoms there were in the atmosphere during every century all the way back through time; but they are starting to work their way back. How they are finding this out is by carbon-14 dating wood from very old trees. The real age of this wood is determined by counting tree rings.[30] In this manner, carbon-14 dating has been checked back more than 7000 years as of 1971.[31] As of 1982, the ring sequence was extended back to about 9000 years ago.

As a result of testing tree rings, it was found that carbon-14 dates had been slightly in error (about 15% off for a 7000 year old specimen) due to the differing rates of atmospheric C-14 production in past ages. However, the observed error was *not* in the direction which would suggest a young earth. What had previously been measured and thought to be a mere 6000 years old, was now known to be about 7000 years old. Now that the direction and amount of this error is known, the information is used to correct modern C-14 dates and thereby make them more accurate.

Other checks have been made still farther back. For example, a C-14 date of 45,000 years was cross checked with one of the uranium dating systems with only 1,500 years of disagreement.[32] Here it cannot be known which of the two dates (or both) is in error. With C-14 and tree rings, it was understood that the error was in the C-14 date and not in the tree ring count. Although by no means conclusive, this check is at least a good sign.

In specimens from as far back in time as 50,000 years, less than one fourth of one percent of the original C-14 still remains. This makes accurate measurement quite difficult. With the present state of the art, carbon-14 dates of greater than 50,000 years are not accurate enough to be useful. It is not expected that

---

[30]A tree will almost always add a single growth ring every year; and of course those scientists doing the counting have been careful to make due provision for both missing and duplicate annual growth rings.

[31]"Carbon 14 and the Prehistory of Europe," by Colin Renfrew, SCIENTIFIC AMERICAN, October 1971, Vol. 225, No. 4, pp. 63-72. In particular, see the chart on pp. 66-67.

[32]Ascent to Civilization, John Gowlett, C. 1984, Alfred A. Knopf Inc., N.Y., p. 199. These two results differ by less than 4%.

the C-14 method will ever be refined to a level where it can be used to date material older than 100,000 years.[33]

A specimen becomes too old to be dated by the C-14 method when most of its C-14 has decayed away. Coal, for example, has virtually no C-14 remaining. This means that it is impossible to assign a date to coal using this method – except to say that it must be older than C-14's useful range. It is just not possible to calculate how much older.

In summary, with a reasonable amount of caution, and with moderate corrections for known past variations, carbon-14 can be a useful method for dating organic specimens as old as 9,000 years with a high level of confidence. The underlying assumptions can all be tested this far back. At present, the method can be extended to an upper limit of about 50,000 years ago with increasingly reduced confidence.

The Dating Gap

There is a period called "the dating gap" which is considered very difficult to date. It extends from where C-14 drops off to where the potassium-argon method becomes useful – about half a million years ago. Techniques for dating this period are still under development.[34] For the present, we will do well to be suspicious of dates which fall into this time period.

Potassium-Argon

For dates older than about half a million years, potassium-argon starts to become an effective way to date volcanic materials. The way this method works is that radioactive potassium-40 (potassium is a common mineral element) decays into argon-40 (argon is an inert gas). The argon will become trapped[35] inside the rock crystals where the potassium was. The

---

[33]Ibid p. 86.

[34]Ibid p. 86.

[35]Even if some argon does escape, this would make the sample appear younger, not older than it actually was; less argon means less age. Although this will not weaken the present argument, it can still be a problem for

decay mechanism is similar to carbon-14's but it happens at a much slower rate;[36] it takes 1.3 billion years for half of the potassium-40 to change into argon. This is one reason why potassium-argon (K-Ar) is only useful for such old dates.

Another property of K-Ar dating is that a volcano must erupt to reset its clock to zero. Because this does not happen very often in most parts of the world, it is not always possible to use K-Ar dating to assign precise dates. Individual eruptions in one location might be hundreds of thousands or many millions of years apart.

When a volcanic sample is heated to melting (this is the condition of hot lava from an erupting volcano), all of the argon-40 is driven out of it.[37] Because argon is inert, it cannot react with or combine to hot volcanic rock at all. Instead, the argon is boiled completely out of the rock and released into the atmosphere. This means that every time a volcano erupts and ejects hot lava or ash, the lava and ash will have no argon in them. This is how a volcano resets the K-Ar clock; no argon means that no time has elapsed since the eruption which ejected the particular sample.

This is certainly true at the earth's surface; but if a volcano erupts far beneath the surface of the ocean, the tremendous pressure at this depth can prevent the argon from completely escaping. The resulting error can be more than 10 million years of false age when the water is a few miles deep.[38] Because of this, we should allow for the possibility that underwater K-Ar dates might appear significantly older than they really are. However, this is not a problem with surface volcanos; nor does

---

scientists. See <u>Lucy: the Beginnings of Humankind,</u> by Donald Johanson and Maitland Edey, C. 1981, Warner Books, N.Y., pp. 188, 192.

[36]Actually, the process for potassium-40 is slightly more complicated; there are two decay mechanisms involved: electron capture into argon-40 and beta decay into calcium-40; but this second product is not normally used in dating samples.

[37]<u>Lucy: the Beginnings of Humankind</u>, by Donald Johanson and Maitland Edey, C. 1981, Warner Books, N.Y., pp. 190, 192.

[38]"Deep-Ocean Basalts: Inert Gas Content and Uncertainties in Age Dating," C.S. Noble and J.J. Naughton, SCIENCE, October 11, 1968, Vol. 162, No. 3850, pp. 265-266.

this amount of error appear to be very significant when one is dealing with ages ranging in the hundreds of millions of years.

From the time of the eruption onward, any argon in an uncontaminated sample has to have been produced by decaying potassium — at least for surface volcanos. By measuring the amount of potassium-40 in the sample and the amount of argon which is released when the sample is re-heated in a laboratory, it can be determined how long ago a particular volcanic eruption occurred. The more argon present, the longer ago it happened.

Because of the small amounts of argon involved and because of the possibility of some contamination,[39] K-Ar dates are usually believed to be accurate only to within about plus or minus 100,000 years. The best dates can be as close as ±50,000 years[40] but errors approaching a million years are to be occasionally expected when scientists get careless. Although errors of this size are of great concern to scientists working in the field, they will not be too much of a problem for us here. Even these great errors are not too significant when one is dealing with things that happened millions of years ago; three million years with a million years' worth of possible error is still at least two million years.

The K-Ar method is useful for determining the ages of the various strata in a segment of the geologic column. When a volcano erupts, ash is spread over a large area of ground. Later, it may become buried. Thus, volcanic ash can often be found between layers of earth. If a pure sample of that ash can be analyzed, then a real date can be assigned to that level of the column. A scientist will know that any fossil found "below"[41] that level is older than the ash. That fossil must have been buried before the volcano erupted or the ash would not have fallen on layers above it. Likewise the scientist knows that fossils which he finds in layers "above" the ash are more recent. Occasionally

---

[39]A small amount of contamination is almost inevitable because there is some argon present in the atmosphere.

[40]Lucy: the Beginnings of Humankind, by Donald Johanson and Maitland Edey, C. 1981, Warner Books, N.Y., p. 188. Older dates are likely to have greater errors.

[41]The terms "above" and "below" refer to the time when the earth's layers were originally laid down. In some cases, such as when faulting occurs, the earth can shift around and make these directions difficult to discern.

a scientist will be lucky enough to find a fossil sandwiched closely between two datable layers and can know the age of his find quite accurately.[42]

Young-earth creationists often claim that the geological time scale was worked out by evolutionists before radioactive dating was even invented – that the presently assigned dates, therefore, really have nothing to do with radioactive dating methods at all.[43] This claim ignores the fact that when radioactive dating did become available, it was discovered that the first guesses (presumably based on evolutionary assumptions) had been greatly in error and so they were corrected. For example, the Miocene, formerly thought to have begun nine hundred thousand years ago, was found to have begun more than twenty million years earlier![44] Here the truth was twenty times more ancient than the original estimate! The presently accepted dates have very little in common with the earlier ones.

Potassium-argon dating can also be useful in determining how various parts of the earth have moved around during past ages. The continental masses are gradually drifting around, sometimes colliding with each other, sometimes splitting apart. As a result, over the years the "geologic column" has been broken into many large and small pieces. Also wind and water erode away some top layers, leaving others, and deposit the rubble elsewhere. Dating a vertical sequence of lava flows can help a geologist to determine how the various pieces fit together. Of course there is a good deal of other evidence to help him – such as the visible presence of fault lines.

Working out the particular geology of an area is always a necessary first step which must be taken before any fossils can be reliably dated using the potassium-argon method.[45] This can be either an easy or difficult task depending on how broken up the terrain is or how visible the various layers are. At many

---

[42]Lucy: the Beginnings of Humankind, by Donald Johanson and Maitland Edey, C. 1981, Warner Books, N.Y., p. 116.

[43]For example, Scientific Creationism, Ed. by Henry M. Morris Ph.D., C. 1974, Master Books, El Cajon, Ca., p. 133.

[44]Lucy: the Beginnings of Humankind, by Donald Johanson and Maitland Edey, C. 1981, Warner Books, N.Y., pp. 95-96.

[45]Ibid pp. 114-115, 152-153. See for examples of contrasting geologies.

places such as the Grand Canyon, where all of the layers are orderly and exposed for observation, this task is simple. At other places, where faulting has displaced the layers and they are only sporadically visible, the task can be quite difficult. Of course, the volcanic materials themselves can always be dated without knowledge of the surrounding geology.

In summary, potassium-argon is a useful method for dating volcanic materials which are older than about 500,000 years and which were erupted from surface volcanos. To get accurate dates, care must be taken that samples are not contaminated. Accuracy will not be better than ±50,000 years; in extreme cases, it can be much worse. If fossils are to be dated by this method, the surrounding geology must be understood. Volcanic materials which were erupted into deep oceans might date much older than they really are.

Conclusions

Although it is freely admitted that there are a great many questions for which scientists have not yet produced convincing answers, the question of whether or not the universe is young is certainly *not* one of them. God's creation consistently bears witness of its old age. There are many ways of assigning dates which have not been discussed here. These include the fission-track method and paleomagnetism.[46] Careful scientists cross-check their dates with as many of the different ways as possible. What they have found is repeated confirmation (within normal experimental limitations) of the very old dates for the various events of the earth's history.

This author has spent a great deal of time investigating various young-earth arguments − chasing down original sources − reviewing the methodology used etc. − and has never found a single argument which stood up when studied in context with other scientific evidence. All of the young-earth arguments which he has examined contain mistakes. Here are just a few more examples:

---

[46]Ibid pp. 200-205.

▶ That the earth's magnetic field is steadily decaying; it would have been too intense in the past if the earth is old: See <u>Origin and Destiny of the Earth's Magnetic Field</u>, by Dr. Thomas G. Barnes, 1973, Institute for Creation Research, San Diego, Ca.

The evidence shows that, over the long term, it is not decaying; in fact it periodically reverses direction. This would be impossible with a simple decay phenomenon. See <u>Palaeomagnetism, Principles and Applications in Geology, Geophysics and Archaeology</u>, D.H. Tarling, C. 1983, Chapman and Hall, London, pp. 181-187. Also, tree rings keep running records of C-14 concentrations in the atmosphere which relate to the intensity of the earth's magnetic field; but their record shows that the actual variation in C-14 concentrations, since 7000 years ago, disagrees radically with what this young-earth theory predicts. See "Carbon 14 and the Prehistory of Europe," by Colin Renfrew, SCIENTIFIC AMERICAN, October 1971, Vol. 225, No. 4, pp. 66, 67.

▶ That rivers constantly wash minerals into the oceans; there is too little salt etc. in the oceans if the earth is old: See <u>Scientific Creationism</u>, Ed. by Henry M. Morris Ph.D., C. 1974, Master Books, El Cajon, Ca., pp. 153-155.

This argument considers influx rates only. It ignores many aspects of the ocean's chemistry which remove minerals (for example: precipitation, strong sorption process, and nodule formation) and also that plate motion periodically sweeps the sea floor clear. If this argument were valid, the amount of aluminum in the ocean would prove that the earth was only 100 years old. This would mean that the Civil War had never really been fought. But, of course, this argument is not valid. Ocean water does not simply result from concentration of in-flowing river waters. See <u>Marine Chemistry</u>, by R.A. Horne, C. 1969, Wiley-Inter-science, N.Y., p. 424; <u>Continents in Collision</u>, by Russell Miller, C. 1983, Time-Life Books, Alexandria, Virginia, pp. 80-82; and <u>The Cambridge Encyclopedia of Earth Sciences</u>, Ed. David G. Smith Ph.D., C. 1981, Crown Publishers Inc. / Cambridge University Press, N.Y., p. 60.

▶ That there is insufficient meteoric dust mixed into the earth's crust if it is old: See <u>Scientific Creationism</u>, Ed. by Henry M. Morris Ph.D., C. 1974, Master Books, El Cajon, Ca., pp. 151-153.

As we have seen, there is 1000 times less meteoric influx to the earth than was assumed for that calculation. There are also processes at work removing this dust. Soil is constantly being washed into the oceans, deposited on the sea floors, and then the sea floors themselves are continuously being pulled down into the earth's mantle. Meteoric elements are "siderophile" (combine with iron) and so they are ultimately scavenged into the earth's core. See <u>The Cambridge Encyclopedia of Earth Sciences</u>, Ed. David G. Smith Ph.D., C. 1981, Crown Publishers Inc. / Cambridge University Press, N.Y., pp. 33, 58.

▶ That scientists use circular reasoning to assign dates to the geologic layers and the fossils which they contain – dating each by the other:

This certainly was a problem back before the development of radioactive dating techniques, though it is not really much of a problem today; but scientists are human and may, even today, occasionally fall into this trap. According to proper procedure, index fossils are not used unless they have first been consistently tied to a single radioactive date range. This is not circular reasoning. For a valid (although still controversial) application of index fossils, see <u>Lucy: the Beginnings of Humankind</u>, by Donald Johanson and Maitland Edey, C. 1981, Warner Books, N.Y., p. 238.

▶ It used to be argued that the sun is shrinking too rapidly – that it would have been too big in the past if the earth is old; but this argument is presently losing support. See <u>It's a Young World After All, Exciting Evidences for Recent Creation</u>, Paul D. Ackerman, C. 1986, Baker Book House, Grand Rapids, Michigan 49506, pp. 61-63.

The measuring technique was changed (giving the sun a different *apparent* size); but the sun's actual size seems to have stayed the same. If the sun had really been as much larger in the past as was claimed, *some historically recorded total eclipses would have been impossible*. See "The Consistency of the Solar Diameter Over the Past 250 Years," by John H. Parkinson, Leslie V. Morrison and F. Richard Stephenson. NATURE, December 11, 1980, Vol. 288, pp. 548, 549.

▶ Comets are short lived; there are too many of them still orbiting the sun if the solar system is old. See Scientific Creationism, Ed. by Henry M. Morris Ph.D., C. 1974, Master Books, El Cajon, Ca., p. 158.

New comets are continuously being introduced into our solar system from out beyond Pluto's orbit. When far away from the sun, comets are not short lived. See Mysteries of the Universe, Nigel Henbest, C. 1981, Van Nostrand Reinhold Company, N.Y., p. 22.

This author has found oversights or mistakes in all of the young-earth "proofs" which he has investigated. They simply do not agree with the creation's evidence.[47] Because so many different arguments have been given, the time cannot possibly be taken to systematically refute them all here. It is hoped that any readers who are still unconvinced that the earth is old will be like the Bereans of Acts 17:11 and will carefully examine the evidence themselves. There are plenty of libraries full of data which are free for the using.

---

[47]Incidentally, these refuted examples prove that the claims of creationists can be "falsified" (proven wrong) in the same sense that any other scientific theory can be. This refutes the claim which is sometimes made by non-creationists that they cannot be falsified and are therefore not to be considered "scientific" theories. For example, see Hen's Teeth and Horse's Toes, Stephen Jay Gould, C. 1983, W.W. Norton & Co., N.Y., p. 256. In this sense, creationist's theories can be considered to be scientific; but, in any case, the young-earth theories are certainly wrong.

Chapter 6:
Understanding Genesis Chapter One

"By wisdom the Lord laid the earth's foundations, by understanding he set the heavens in place; by his knowledge the deeps were divided, and the clouds let drop the dew."

—Proverbs 3:19, 20.

Although the "days" of the first chapter of Genesis can be interpreted to allow for a very old universe, this won't do any good unless the rest of that chapter makes sense in this context. God's creation account brings up many other questions which must also be answered. Here the various statements made in Genesis 1 will be examined in the combined light of what the Bible says and what scientists have been able to learn about God's creation.

As will be seen, the rocks and stars are rich in very detailed information; they say a great deal about their origins and their Creator. Unfortunately, the Bible contains very few total pages about the beginning; and what it does relate is much less detailed than we would like. While it will be comparatively easy to decipher what God's creation is telling us, it will not always be so simple to grasp exactly what His Bible is saying here.

This chapter will present an attempt to correlate the first chapter of Genesis with the universe. It is *not* the intent to make dogmatic statements about what Genesis actually means; instead, mere possibilities will be suggested. The scientific evidence will occasionally expose an incorrect interpretation of scripture; but it can never prove that any understanding is correct.

Genesis 1 will be examined very closely. Where it is scientifically possible, *how* God worked will be examined in addition to just *what* He did. Although at times God left the scientists utterly without a clue as to how He worked, at other times He left so much evidence of His methodology that a determined atheist can imagine the processes could have occurred even without God's hand on them. As God's Bible reflects the individual styles of its many human recorders, so also His universe retains the marks of His various channels of creation – sometimes supernatural, other times quite natural. In all cases, in both God's Bible and in His universe, we see God's wisdom revealed through the ultimate result.

Creationists often emphasize God's power and authority and neglect His wisdom, knowledge and understanding. As Proverbs 3:19, 20 (quoted at the beginning of this chapter) tells us, these three played an important role in the creation. We often erroneously picture God as a sort of powerful magician who speaks a single magic word, then steps back and the heavens simply obey. According to this image, God does not reason out each of the incomprehensible myriad details of what He is doing. The actual working out of those minute elements of design is somehow left up to the "magic" itself; but, of course, God *is* the "magic." It is He who works out every microscopic detail.

Psalm 33:6 states: "By the word of the Lord were the heavens made." Here God's creative agency is metaphorically described as the "word." (In John 1:1, Jesus is similarly described as the "word.") Psalm 33:9: continues "For he spoke, and it came to be; he commanded, and it stood firm." Once God has spoken something, it is certainly as good as done; but this is different from saying that God merely spoke the command, then sat back and watched some other creative agency deliver the results. God created the universe by Himself (Isaiah 44:24). God does have the power to "speak things into existence." But we must remember that He also *is* that power; He is the one who does as well as the one who speaks. God worked out every single detail Himself. He "made the earth by His power," but He also "founded the world by his wisdom." (Jeremiah 10:12, 51:15).

This picture of God's methodology is supported by the Hebrew wording of Genesis 1:1. The word there for created is "bara" which, according to Gesenius, means "To cut, to carve out, to form by cutting."[1] For example, both the N.I.V. and N.A.S. translated this word "cut" in Ezekiel 23:47. It is commonly taught that "bara" means something like "to create out of nothing." Apparently it does not. This word appears to speak of God's craftsmanship rather than of His power to create matter from nothing. Of course, it is still true that God actually did create the universe starting from nothing – at least from nothing which is a visible part of this universe (Hebrews 11:3).

God once gave Job a brief and highly figurative lecture on how much attention to detail was required to create the universe:

"Where were you when I laid the earth's foundation? Tell me, if you understand. Who marked off its dimensions? Surely you know! Who stretched a measuring line across it? On what were its footings set, or who laid its cornerstone – while the morning stars sang together and all the angels shouted for joy? ..."

– Job 38:4-7.

Today, scientists are able to read some of these details. Like Job, we can never really appreciate just how much was involved in making the universe, but what we can learn from science will help us to come to a better understanding of who God really is.

---

[1] Gesenius' Hebrew-Chaldee Lexicon to the Old Testament, C. 1979, Baker Book House Co., Grand Rapids, Michigan, p. 138, (entry #1254).

Day 1: The Universe

Genesis 1:1

"In the beginning God created the heavens and the earth."

As recently as a hundred years ago, writing this book would not have been an easy task. At that time it was taught in physics courses that matter could neither be created nor destroyed. If this book had been written at that time, it would have been difficult to resolve the resulting conflict: If matter could not be created, then it must have always existed and there could have been no beginning. At that time the only agreement which could possibly be reached would be that if a creation were possible, it certainly would have taken God to do it.

Modern physics now confirms what Bible believing Christians knew by faith all along. Einstein supplied the necessary relationship between matter and energy[2] and later the Heisenberg uncertainty principle supplied a possible relation between energy and time. Scientists are now quite willing to concede that a moment of creation was possible. Other evidence even dictates the *necessity* of a creation. The famous second law of thermodynamics (Boltzmann/Kelvin) establishes that the universe must not have always existed or it would have run down to a dead stop before now.[3] Hubble's correlation between red shifts and distances to stars, and the consequent rate of expansion for the universe, even indicates a rough estimate for the time of its creation.[4]

As Hubble's observations showed, the more distant galaxies have proportionally greater red shifts. (Red shift is a measure of how rapidly a distant galaxy is traveling away from us.) This

---

[2]Although discovery of the equivalence between matter and energy ($E = mc^2$) is universally attributed to Albert Einstein, not all sources agree. See Evolution From Space, by Fred Hoyle and Chandra Wickramasinghe, C. 1981, Simon & Schuster Inc., N.Y., p. 10.

[3]Mechanics, Heat, and Sound, by Francis Weston Sears, C. 1950, Addison-Wesley Publishing Company, Inc., Reading, Massachusetts, p. 464.

[4]God and the Astronomers, by Robert Jastrow, C. 1978, W.W. Norton and Company, Inc., N.Y., P. 47.

means that all galaxies are moving away from a single point in space – that they all must have started from there at the same time. All of the matter in the universe is behaving as if it were the debris left over from a colossal explosion which once happened at that point. Using his limited information, Hubble calculated that this explosion must have occurred about two billion years ago.[5] Later refinements corrected this estimate to the presently established range of fifteen to twenty billion years.

Penzias and Wilson's measurement of the universe's background radiation confirms a very violent beginning at about this time.[6] More recently, evidence from nucleosynthesis has quantitatively confirmed some of the fine detail concerning this event[7] which cosmologists call the "big bang."

Although correct in substance, the big bang theory is often couched in terminology which assumes atheism. This, unfortunately, makes Christians reject it without even considering it logically. An atheist will attempt to present the moment of creation as if it were a completely "random accident" – one which, by "lucky coincidence," started a chain reaction of cause and effect that ultimately fell together into the Sistine Chapel and Marilyn Monroe among other wonders. But the "big bang" requires neither unguided randomness nor an accident. Besides, even those processes which appear random to humans are under God's control. "The lot is cast into the lap, but its every decision is from the Lord." (Proverbs 16:33).

Design and purpose in the guiding hand of an intelligent creator are consistent with the evidence for this cosmic-scaled explosion; but the random-accident scenario leaves an endless list of unanswered questions such as: How was the wildly expanding fireball sculpted into the universe's galaxies? How was the immense gravitational attraction of all this tightly-

---

[5]Compounding the roughness and incompleteness of Hubble's early measurements, was the fact that one of his assumptions was also in error. See "The Andromeda Galaxy" by Paul W. Hodge, SCIENTIFIC AMERICAN, January 1981, Vol. 244, No. 1, pp. 95-96.

[6]God and the Astronomers, by Robert Jastrow, C. 1978, W.W. Norton and Company, Inc., N.Y., pp. 14-21

[7]"Particle Accelerators Test Cosmological Theory," by David N. Schramm and Gary Steigman, SCIENTIFIC AMERICAN, June 1988, Vol. 258, No. 6, pp. 68, 69.

concentrated mass overcome?[8] And, what could possibly have set it off in the first place?[9]

In any case, the moment of creation has been conceded. Modern science has come as far as giving us a description of how the universe began which even matches the details of the Biblical account. According to Einstein's laws, before there was any energy or matter in the universe, there could not have been any time or space either.[10] If there was no time "before" this event, then there really was no "before" at all! Although this confuses us, it is no problem for God; His existence is somehow independent of time as it relates to our physical universe.

Time and space cannot exist where there is no matter. This means that the moment of the creation of matter marked the beginning of time and the creation of the "heavens" which we call "space." This sounds very similar to the Bible's, "In the beginning God created the heavens and the earth." (Genesis 1:1). It would be a remarkable match if the Hebrew word for "earth" also referred to cosmic matter in the general sense – the matter from which the earth, stars and planets were ultimately formed. According to Gesenius' lexicon, the word "erets" (translated "earth" here) *did* carry the alternate meaning "element of the earth" to the ancient Hebrews.[11] This means the Biblical and scientific accounts of the first moment of creation match exactly!

---

[8]Under Einstein's laws, the gravitational attraction would have been so intense that time itself would be unable to proceed in a "real" forward direction! Perhaps a unified field theory will, one day soon, throw light on at least this one question.

[9]Those who are uncomfortable with a moment of creation (and hence a creator) have proposed the hypothesis that the universe goes through endless cycles of "big bang" followed by "big crunch" where it collapses again only to be re-exploded in a subsequent "big bang." Even if this hypothesis proves to be true, it does not eliminate the need for a moment of creation anyway because even these cycles will run down; each successive cycle is believed to be comprised of less matter and more energy than the preceding one. See The First Three Minutes, A Modern View of the Origin of the Universe, Updated Edition, Steven Weinberg, C. 1977, 1988, Basic Books, Inc., Publishers, N.Y., pp. 153-154.

[10]See Einstein's Universe, Nigel Calder, C. 1979, The Viking Press, N.Y., pp. 122, 124-125.

[11]Gesenius' Hebrew-Chaldee Lexicon to the Old Testament, C. 1979, Baker Book House Co., Grand Rapids, Michigan, p. 81, (entry #776, definition #6).

Cosmologists tell us that about fifteen or twenty billion years ago, matter, time, and space appeared together with the cosmic "big bang." The energy of this explosion was what caused the creation of the stuff from which stars and planets were later formed (cosmic matter) and sent it spreading in all directions at nearly the speed of light. According to relativity, even "space" itself spreads with the mass of the stars.[12] Notice how this account matches with Jeremiah 10:12:

> "God made the earth by his power; he founded the world by his wisdom and stretched out the heavens by his understanding."

In particular, notice the cause-and-effect connection between matter and energy[13] and how the heavens are spread out. The word "earth" is again translated from "erets" and may again refer to matter in general.

Although in the past science did not seem to bear out Genesis 1:1, at the present time it does so very closely – just so long as we are willing to accept a longer-than-twenty-four-hour interpretation for the creative "days." Scientists now tell us that matter was created under exactly the circumstances which the Bible described thousands of years ago. Of course the scientists have not yet been able to fathom every aspect of God's creation, but they have come a long way.

This confirms some observations made back in the second chapter of this book: Even if science disagrees with theology, that does not necessarily prove that theology is in error. As we know today, theologians were correct in saying, back in the last century, that the universe was created – even when this was still in disagreement with science. Similarly, even if theology appears to be in agreement with science, that does not necessarily prove that we are interpreting the Bible correctly. Interpreters of both scripture and the universe can be wrong at the same time – even

---

[12]Mysteries of the Universe, Nigel Henbest, C. 1981, Van Nostrand Reinhold Co., N.Y., p. 175

[13]Even if we were to insist on technical accuracy and differentiate between "energy" and "power" we would have no trouble here because energy is equivalent to power operating for some period of time. But, of course, it would be silly for us to insist that ancient Hebrew prophets respect present-day technical distinctions in their writings.

when they agree with each other.[14] Remember that the Inquisition used both Scripture and science against Galileo! Truth can be very elusive, no simple approach can always be trusted to lead us in the correct direction.

Genesis 1:2

"Now the Earth was formless and empty, darkness was over the surface of the deep, and the Spirit of God was hovering over the waters."

This verse is also a very interesting one; in fact, it is a subject of much controversy. Creationists sometimes place a huge time gap here in which many things supposedly happened but were not recorded in the Bible. This theory was originally proposed as an attempt to correlate the purported short days of Genesis with the long ones of science. It adds a complication to scriptural interpretation which is totally unnecessary; the "days" of Genesis can refer to long periods of time without the need for invented gaps. Such complications should always be avoided when there is neither a scientific nor Biblical reason for including them.[15]

Back in Genesis 1:1 God created the matter from which the planet earth was later to be formed. Here in verse two, this matter is being formed into a planet. Taking Genesis 1:2 as a literal description of how our solar system (the earth, sun, moon and planets) actually looked as it was being formed, yields good agreement with modern scientific theory concerning this event. If, instead, verse two is taken to describe just the early earth, immediately *following* the formation of our solar system, there is still good agreement with scientific theory. Because both the Biblical and scientific data concerning this event are so vague,

---

[14]It, of course, follows that this author's attempts to correlate present-day scientific theories with the Bible should not be taken too seriously. If science moves on, this book will suffer the same fate as many other past attempts to correlate the Bible with the teachings of men. The only reason why this author has bothered to write it at all is that he is convinced that the scientists have finally stumbled onto some actual truth. Time will judge.

[15]Although it would be an unnecessary digression from the subject to comment on this theory here, the author's opinions are included in Appendix 4 for anyone who is interested.

there is a lot of room for speculation. Some different possibilities will be suggested here.

There are many theories concerning the formation of our solar system and much is still unknown. However, it is agreed by astronomers that solar systems form from clouds of interstellar matter called nebulae.[16] A nebula is a very large shapeless cloud of interstellar gas and dust (cosmic matter) floating in space. In the case of the formation of our own solar system, this cloud is believed to have contained the remains of an ancient star (or stars) which exploded long ago.[17] Eventually, gravitational forces pulled this matter into solid clumps which became our sun and its planets. At first, before the sun ignited, this process would be occurring in the darkness of interstellar space.

This scientific reckoning of the formation of our solar system, from a dark shapeless cloud of space dust, bears a remarkable resemblance to the Bible's, "The earth was formless and empty, darkness was over the surface of the deep." The word "earth" was again translated from "erets" and could therefore refer to the drifting matter of a dark nebula. But there is no reason why this verse could not refer to just the incompletely-formed planet earth which was still in darkness – either owing to the dark cloud of dust still enveloping it or to awaited ignition of the sun.

Continuing with the second verse, "The Spirit of God was hovering over the waters." This is also very rich in possible interpretations. Here emphasis is being shifted from "matter" in general to "water" more specifically; water plays a key role in the creation of life and is the focus of the next few verses. A shift in emphasis at this early stage might imply an early start toward the creation of life; still, there might be different reasons why emphasis was shifted at this point.

The phrase "was hovering" ("moved" in the more familiar King James version) is translated from the Hebrew "rachaph"

---

[16]Mysteries of the Universe, Nigel Henbest, C. 1981, Van Nostrand Reinhold Co., N.Y., pp. 14, 15, 88, 89.

[17]This conclusion is based on the relative abundance of the various elements of the periodic table as they occur in our planetary system. Einstein's Universe, Nigel Calder, C. 1979, The Viking Press, N.Y., p. 17.

which is used only two other places in the entire Bible (Deut. 32:11 and Jer. 23:9). The word means something like "to be moved or affected" as with love or fear.[18] First taking Jer. 23:9, "... My heart is broken within me; all my bones tremble, ..." Here the word "tremble" is translated from the Hebrew "rachaph." In this case the one who is speaking (God) is being moved by distress. Deuteronomy 32:11 gives a nicer picture. "Like an eagle that stirs up its nest, and hovers over its young,..." Here the Hebrew "rachaph" was translated as "hovers." (This is also how the N.I.V. translated this word in Genesis 1:2.) This time it is used in a sense similar to a hen brooding over her eggs – being moved as with love. This might be what is intended in Genesis 1:2, but as we will see, the Jeremiah usage might also be the truth. God may have intended both shades of meaning at the same time.

There are other sources of uncertainty in this verse. The word "Spirit" (translated in Genesis 1:2 from the Hebrew "ruach") could also be translated as "breath" or "wind." If "wind" were the intended meaning, then the phrase "of God" would probably take on another shade of meaning, more like "mighty" or "violent."[19] This would imply the less gentle understanding of "rachaph" implied by Jeremiah. A mightily raging wind could certainly be described as being moved with "emotion." This phrase could be translated, "and the wind of God raged on the waters." This would not necessarily mean that the "brooded" understanding implied by Deuteronomy is wrong; if God meant to accomplish a creative step with His mighty wind, it would still represent a loving God "brooding" over His creation.

Scientifically, the birth of stars (and their planets) can be initiated by a cosmic compression wave in the nebular medium.[20] This wave could be described as a wind of incomprehensible power – one which would cause the birth of our sun. On the other hand, if this verse does not describe the

---

[18]Gesenius' Hebrew-Chaldee Lexicon to the Old Testament, C. 1979, Baker Book House Co., Grand Rapids, Michigan, p. 766, (entry #7363).

[19]See The Genesis Debate, Ronald Youngblood, C. 1986, Thomas Nelson Publishers, Nashville, pp. 113-118, the "no" argument.

[20]"The Milky Way Galaxy," by Bart J. Bok, SCIENTIFIC AMERICAN, March 1981, Vol. 244, No. 3, p. 115.

formation of the solar system but only describes the early planet earth, then "wind" might refer to a great burst of solar wind from a giant sun flare. Scientists believe that such a blast may have cleared away much of the nebular dust.[21] Under this interpretation, the sun might have already been shining before this time, but its light would not yet be visible from earth because of an excessive amount of surrounding dust. A strong enough blast would clear this dust away. Notice that under either of these two interpretations, we might expect light to become visible immediately following the blast of "wind."

Genesis 1:3

"And God said, 'Let there be light,' and there was light."

As explained, our solar system, including the sun, the moon, the earth and the other planets, was originally formed from nebular space-dust falling together into clumps. The sun was by far the largest clump and, according to the laws of thermodynamics, would therefore be much hotter and under much more pressure than the planets were.

If you have ever had an opportunity to use an old-fashioned hand-operated tire pump, you can appreciate how air gets hotter when it is compressed. The pump can get so hot that it becomes uncomfortable to hold. The forces involved in a forming star are much greater and the temperatures thus generated are great indeed! When the material of the forming star (which is mostly hydrogen) becomes hot enough, the star will ignite[22] – quite literally as a giant continuously-burning hydrogen bomb!

When this happens, there is light. The nuclear fusion reaction takes place way down in the center of the newly formed star. Eventually its energy will reach the surface and the star will begin to shine. Genesis 1:3 may describe the creation of the sun

---

[21]Origins: a Skeptic's Guide to the Creation of Life on Earth, Robert Shapiro, C. 1986, Summit Books, N.Y., p. 96.

[22]God and the Astronomers, Robert Jastrow, C. 1978, W.W. Norton and Company, inc., N.Y., pp. 106-107. The temperature at which a star will kindle is twenty million degrees Fahrenheit.

or it may describe a time when the sun's light first became visible to the earth owing to the removal of some nebular dust. Either way, God created the sun during His first "day." As will be explained later, another event is described during God's fourth "day." Scientists date this event – the creation of the sun and planets – at about 4.5 billion years ago.

Genesis 1:4, 5

"God saw that the light was good, and he separated the light from the darkness. God called the light 'day,' and the darkness he called 'night.' And there was evening and there was morning – the first day."

As was briefly mentioned, stars generate a "wind" of sorts. A new star will sporadically flare and generate this "wind" in bursts. After a star has settled into a stable routine, this "stellar wind" (comprised of elementary particles which "blow" away from it at about a million miles per hour) also stabilizes.[23] The stellar wind eventually blows the remaining dust away from the solar system; but at the moment of the star's ignition, there would still be plenty of interplanetary dust present. At first, there may have been enough to keep the planets in darkness.

With time, there would have been less dust. At some point the solar system must have merely been a hazy place; sunlight would have bounced around in a moderate amount of interplanetary dust. Hence, the first sunlight would have reached the earth from all sides. Even the back side of the earth would be illuminated by light reflected off this dust. Adding to this, the earth was initially very hot. It may have been hot enough to glow and emit some light of its own – although it never reached a high enough temperature to become a star like the sun did.[24]

---

[23]The Hebrew phrase "God *saw* that the light was good" could be translated "God *saw to it that* the light was good." This might mean that God had to bring the light under control before it was what he had in mind. See Gesenius' Hebrew-Chaldee Lexicon to the Old Testament, C. 1979, Baker Book House Co., Grand Rapids, Michigan, p. 749, (entry #7200, definition 2e).

[24]As mentioned earlier, size determines whether a body will ultimately become a hot star or a cool planet. See Mysteries of the Universe, Nigel Henbest, C. 1981, Van Nostrand Reinhold Co., N.Y., p. 93.

These initial conditions would have produced light on both sides of the earth at the same time; there would have been no night.

Genesis 1:4, 5 tells us that God separated the light from the darkness; the scientific account tells us He did this by further clearing of the interplanetary dust with the solar wind – and possibly by cooling the earth's surface. At present, there is scarcely any dust or debris left floating in our part of space at all – just a few atoms per cubic inch and an occasional meteor, comet or asteroid.

When this dust finally blew away, the light from the sun hit the earth directly as it does today. This meant one side of the turning planet was bathed in the sun's light while the other side was in the earth's own shadow. When the earth's surface cooled, it could not emit light so the shadow side was truly in darkness. Hence there was the separation of the day from the night. Again, God's universe tells the same story His Biblical account does.

Day 2: Separation of the Waters

Genesis 1:6-8

"And God said, 'Let there be an expanse between the waters to separate water from water.' So God made the expanse and separated the water under the expanse from the water above it. And it was so. God called the expanse 'sky.' And there was evening, and there was morning – the second day."

Here the word "sky" is translated from the Hebrew "shamayim." Although "shamayim" is the same Hebrew word which was translated "heavens" back in verse one, those "heavens" are different from the "sky" which God is creating here. Remember, the same word can sometimes be used to mean two different things even in the same Biblical passage. In verse one, God created the heavens which we call "space"; here He is creating the heavens which we call the sky.

As mentioned previously, the early earth was quite hot. Initially it reached temperatures which may have been hot enough to melt rocks.[25] The center of the earth is hot enough to melt rocks even today; but it is kept heated by energy from radioactive minerals.[26] The earth's surface did cool with time though. First the earth cooled sufficiently to form a solid crust. Later, it became cool enough that volcanic steam could condense upon it into liquid water.[27] This appears to be what is written about in verses six through eight. Instead of having one big cloud of steam (water in gas form) surrounding the planet, water condensed onto its surface (the waters below) while a great mass of clouds (the waters above) remained above the growing "expanse" of air.

This expanse of air was mostly nitrogen, carbon dioxide and water vapor which had accumulated from volcanic activity. From the absence of heavy inert gasses in our present atmosphere, scientists conclude that the earth's original atmosphere must have been stripped off – possibly by the same solar flare that cleared the solar system of dust.[28]

We see this from a slightly different perspective in another Biblical reference which describes the same event:

"By wisdom the Lord laid the earth's foundations, by understanding he set the heavens in place; by his knowledge the deeps were divided, and the clouds let drop the dew."

– Proverbs 3:19, 20.

---

[25]See The Panda's Thumb, S.J. Gould, C. 1980, W.W. Norton & Co., N.Y., p. 218.

[26]The radioactive uranium, thorium and potassium in the earth's interior are estimated to produce about 9.5×10^{20} Joules/year of heat energy. This is sufficient to keep it quite warm. See The Cambridge Encyclopedia of Earth Sciences, Ed. David G. Smith Ph.D., C. 1981, Crown Publishers Inc. / Cambridge University Press, N.Y., p. 151.

[27]The original water was volcanic steam. After the earth cooled, this steam condensed into surface water. See Marine Chemistry, R.A. Horne, C. 1969, Wiley-Interscience, N.Y., p. 421.

[28]One theory is that this was done by the same solar flare which cleared the solar system: Origins: a Skeptic's Guide to the Creation of Life on Earth, Robert Shapiro, C. 1986, Summit Books, N.Y., p. 96. Another theory is that a geological upheaval stripped the original atmosphere: The Cambridge Encyclopedia of Earth Sciences, Ed. David G. Smith Ph.D., C. 1981, Crown Publishers Inc. / Cambridge University Press, N.Y., p. 260.

This description contains more detail concerning the division[29] of the deeps (waters);[30] here the waters above (as identified in Genesis) are described as clouds which drop dew to form the waters below.

Again there is good agreement between what the Bible tells us God did and what scientific understanding tells us happened. Scientific understanding is finally converging upon the Biblical account which, remarkably, was composed thousands of years ago. Of course God was there and He knew what happened when He created the world. No one else could have known until this century.

Although scarcely worth mentioning today, the Hebrew word "raqia," translated "expanse" in Genesis 1:6, was in times past a source of confusion. Theology, from around the time of the translation of the King James Bible (and before), seriously regarded the "expanse" as a physical dome which held liquid water up above the sky;[31] hence the translation "firmament" in the King James Version. In verses such as Genesis 7:11 where it figuratively says, "The windows of heaven were opened" (K.J.V.), those theologians envisioned literal windows opening in the dome of the sky and spilling the waters through. That, of course, is not how God causes rain!

There was actually some justification for this historic misinterpretation as there is today for modern mistakes. The root of "raqia" means to spread out by beating – as one might hammer out a bowl from a piece of copper.[32] It was as easy to take this word to mean a sky-size inverted physical bowl which has been beaten into shape as to simply take the idea of a separation or spreading. In fact, without the realization that the waters above could hold themselves aloft in the form of thick clouds, it would be much easier to imagine something physical supporting them.

Of course modern translations reflect this more scientifically correct understanding. The word "expanse" is now used instead

---

[29]Gesenius' Hebrew-Chaldee Lexicon to the Old Testament, C. 1979, Baker Book House Co., Grand Rapids, Michigan, p. 135, (entry #1234).

[30]Ibid p. 857, (entry #8415).

[31]Ibid p. 780, (entry #7549).

[32]Ibid p. 780, (entry #7554).

of the less correct "firmament." There is really nothing new about scientists aiding theologians in Biblical interpretation and translation; it has been going on for quite some time.

Day 3: Dry Land and Plants

Genesis 1:9, 10

"And God said, 'let the water under the sky be gathered to one place, and let dry ground appear.' And it was so. God called the dry ground 'land,' and the gathered waters he called 'seas.' And God saw that it was good."

When the water first condensed onto the young planet's surface, the earth was still very smooth and it was possible for the oceans to cover it entirely. This is because the earth, as a whole, actually behaves more like a liquid mass than as a solid ball. Liquids will not form mountains or valleys very well. Scientists believe that the earth actually was, at one time, completely covered by a shallow sea. At that time, the only solid matter which might occasionally have broken the water's surface would have been volcanic islands.[33]

Although it is not presently known exactly how it happened, geologists tell us that by 2.5 billion years ago, the more-or-less rigid continental masses had formed.[34] These masses, being made of relatively light-weight rock, floated on top of other rock which was heavier.[35] This is similar to how a marshmallow floats in hot chocolate or how aluminum floats in liquid mercury. In this way, the continents were able to reach above the surface of the ocean (see illustration). The phrase "let the dry ground appear" seems to speak of this time when the continents first formed.

---

[33]See Origins: a Skeptic's Guide to the Creation of Life on Earth, Robert Shapiro, C. 1986, Summit Books, N.Y., p. 93.

[34]See The Cambridge Encyclopedia of Earth Sciences, Ed. David G. Smith Ph.D., C. 1981, Crown Publishers Inc. / Cambridge University Press, N.Y., pp. 161, 162.

[35]See Continents in Collision, Russell Miller, C. 1983, Time-Life Books, Alexandria, Virginia, pp. 43, 129.

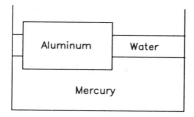

Although aluminum will not float in water, it will float in mercury. It will float high enough to break through a layer of water. The continents do not float on the oceans but they do float on heavier rocks.

There is no reason to be concerned that God did not say that the waters were gathered together into several different oceans as they appear today; the earth has not always looked just like it does right now. According to the well-established theory of plate tectonics, the continents ride on various plates of rock which make up the earth's surface. The center of the earth is a very active environment and it constantly pushes these plates around. Where these plates collide, subduction areas form where matter is drawn back down into the earth's molten center; where they separate, volcanic activity fills in the opening cracks. The continents ride around on these moving masses, sometimes splitting apart or crashing into each other. This motion is a little bit like how foam might float around on the surface of a boiling pot of water.

Geologists tell us that as recently as a couple of hundred million years ago, all of the continents were briefly unified into a single land mass which they refer to as "Pangea."[36] This clumping together is believed to have happened at other earlier times during the earth's past as well. At the time the dry land first appeared, the waters might literally have been gathered into "one place." But the fact that the Bible also refers to the waters as "seas" (plural – as opposed to the singular implied by the phrase "one place") seems to indicate that the actual physical arrangement, over time, may have been somewhat more complicated.

---

[36]Ibid pp. 143, 162.

God also describes the creation and gathering of the seas in Job:

> "Who shut up the sea behind doors when it burst forth from the womb, when I made the clouds its garment and wrapped it in thick darkness. When I fixed limits for it and set its doors and bars in place, when I said, 'This far you may come and no farther; ... '"

>   −Job 38:8-11.

Because there would have been a great deal more water in the clouds back then than there is during any present-day rainstorm, those clouds would have been very dark − hence God's phrase, "wrapped it in thick darkness." Of course the "doors" are figurative (see Job 3:10, Psalm 78:23); they refer to the limits which were imposed on the sea as it was gathered and the dry land appeared.

According to the scientific account, the figurative "womb" from which the primordial sea originally "burst" was the earth's rocks. Whatever atmospheric water the earth had initially was removed when the original atmosphere was stripped. The makings for the present atmosphere and oceans − nitrogen, carbon dioxide and steam − were safely held (chemically bound) in the "womb" of the earth's rocks. Later these elements were released by volcanos and hydrothermal activity.[37] God's words "bursting forth" appear to be quite descriptive of *how* they were released. As explained, this steam later condensed upon the earth's surface to cover it completely with a giant ocean (when the waters below were divided from those above). Here limits are being set for this ocean as the continents appear.

Again, we see a remarkable agreement between the old-earth interpretation of the Biblical account and the scientific account of the earth's beginnings. The Bible is not telling us fairy tales; it appears that the scientists aren't either. Both witnesses appear to have their accounts grounded upon actual truth.

---

[37]Marine Chemistry, R.A. Horne, C. 1969, Wiley-Interscience, N.Y., p. 421.

Genesis 1:11-13

"Then God said, 'Let the land produce vegetation: seed-bearing plants and trees on the land that bear fruit with seed in it, according to their various kinds.' And it was so. The land produced vegetation: plants bearing seed according to their kinds and trees bearing fruit with seed in it according to their kinds. And God saw that it was good. And there was evening, and there was morning – the third day."

As the various created life forms are examined, another minor adjustment to our traditional view of Genesis will become necessary. If the "days" of creation were of indefinite length as has been determined, it is not unreasonable to assume that they might have had indefinite edges as well. As explained back in Chapter 3, the expression "evening and morning" usually carries the idea of "continuously." This could imply that a particular act of creation may have been initiated on a particular "day," although the act could continue and overlap subsequent "days." Thus Genesis might reflect topical as well as chronological organization to some extent; the creation of all plant types could be reported under one heading whether or not every single "kind" was created during that same distinct time slot. If this interpretation is the truth, then the various creative "days" would actually overlap each other somewhat.

There are quite a number of instances where the scientific information demands this. According to the fossil evidence, there are a great many types of plants (described under day three) which God did not create until after He had created some types of fish (day five). For example, the first sharks were created during the Devonian period (about 400 million years ago);[38] but the first flowering plants were not created until more recently (200 million years ago or less).[39] This should not be a surprise; building up a functioning planetary ecosystem is a tricky business and requires that new species be introduced in a

---

[38]The Audubon Society Field Guide to North American Fossils, Ida Thompson, Alfred A. Knopf, N.Y., pp. 759-761.

[39]See Oasis in Space, Earth History from the Beginning, Preston Cloud, C. 1988, W.W. Norton and Company, N.Y., pp. 369, 375-376.

carefully planned order. Flowering plants, for example, require certain insects to pollinate them; God would naturally have held off creating them until His creation was ready for them. We must conclude that at least some of the creative "days" had overlapping edges.

In fact, this same conclusion must be reached however one chooses to interpret the length of the "days" of Genesis. Even under the twenty-four-hour interpretation, the named creative acts must span different creative "days." Scripture tells us that "male and female" humans were created during the sixth "day" (Genesis 1:27); yet God did not create Eve until *after* Adam did many things including naming all the livestock, the birds, and the beasts (Genesis 2:15-22).[40] Adam's activities preceding the creation of Eve must have taken longer than twenty-four hours.

The order in which Genesis presents each of life's forms will be compared with the order in which scientists say that the *first* representatives of each category appeared. This will not be a trivial task for several reasons. First, God did not necessarily group His creatures into the same categories which scientists or even theologians use. Next, scientists get their information from fossils which are hardly ever as plentiful as one would like. Also, it is not known if *first* appearance is even what Genesis addresses. For another possibility, it might address when the *majority* of a category's types were created. These are just a few of the problems which will be encountered.

Of the many living things which God created, the first ones the Bible tells us about are land plants (Genesis 1:11-13). It is tempting to interpret this to mean that the first life was *not* created in the water, as the scientists tell us, but on the land instead. Such a claim is made on page 227 of the book Scientific Creationism.[41] It is more accurate, however, to say that the first created life forms which the Bible *mentions* are those plants which God created upon the land. God may have created other plants in the water before this time.

---

[40]This particular difficulty does not occur under the old-earth interpretation – the sixth day would be long enough to contain the events described.

[41]Scientific Creationism, Ed. Henry M. Morris Ph.D., C. 1974, Master Books, El Cajon, California, p. 227.

In this very concise one-chapter account, God has not told us everything He did! A great deal must have happened of which we have been told nothing. In Genesis 1, God mentions the creation of land plants, aquatic (water living) animals, birds and land animals. There are animals which do not fit into any of these categories – amphibians for example.

Amphibians, such as toads, hatch from eggs in the water, as do fish; but they later undergo modification and relocate to live on the land. Hence they are not exactly water or land animals. Although toads are not specifically mentioned here, or for that matter anywhere else in the Bible, they are certainly among God's creatures.

The Bible does not provide a single clue as to when God might have created amphibians. (The Egyptian plague of frogs in Exodus 8:1-6 doesn't count, of course.) For all we know from scripture, amphibians could have been created before plants were. If scientists are understanding God's creation correctly, then they have provided the missing information; God created the first amphibians between the time He created the first fish and when He created the first true birds.[42]

Blue-green algae, the oldest known plant-like life form which lives in water, is not among those categories which God has named in Genesis 1. In fact, God makes no mention of any aquatic plants there. Therefore we have no scriptural authority for telling the scientists that life did not first appear in the water. All we have a right to say, *if* we are interpreting the Bible correctly, is that the first terrestrial (land living) plants were created before the first aquatic animals were.

Even this will cause some trouble; scientific sources often have this detail the other way around. The oldest known aquatic animals appear about 500-600 million years ago, during an "explosive" episode of creation called the Cambrian period. By comparison, the oldest *known* terrestrial plants do not appear in

---

[42]Amphibians did crawl out of the primordial waters then, just as they still crawl from ponds today. They are cited in biology textbooks as an "evolutionary link" between fish and reptiles as if fish, by their own pioneering spirit, were able to take over the continents. It does *not* follow from the fact that God created an animal (like a frog) which can leave the water to live on the land that evolution is true.

the fossil record until about 400 million years ago.[43] Although scientists do not *know* of any terrestrial plants which preceded aquatic animals, such plants may have existed anyhow.

A lack of fossil evidence does not prove that a particular life form did not exist. In the first place, plants do not often have hard parts and therefore do not fossilize very well.[44] This causes the fossil evidence to be misleading.[45] Next, fossils are much more likely to form on sea floors where sediments are piling up than on the dry land from where those sediments are being washed away.[46] This makes any terrestrial fossils rare. Furthermore, as far back in time as is now being considered, scientists regard the fossil record in general as being very sketchy.[47]

If some terrestrial plants did precede the first aquatic animals, it is not at all clear that there should be any evidence of them; it is improbable that they would have been found in the fossil record. Scientists know from geological evidence that the bulk of the continental crust had formed by 2.5 billion years ago;[48] but what may or may not have been living on that dry land has not yet been seen in the fossil record preceding about 400 million years ago.

Because of this lack of actual evidence, there is some disagreement between sources as to what was happening up on

---

[43]It is at least well established that *aquatic* plant-like life, algae for example, had been around long before the oldest known animals.

[44]They have no bones or shells; however, seeds fossilize better than most plant parts do.

[45]The Cambridge Encyclopedia of Earth Sciences, Ed. David G. Smith Ph.D., C. 1981, Crown Publishers Inc. / Cambridge University Press, N.Y., p. 383. This source explains that the poor fossilability of plants leads to erroneous conclusions about their history. See also Human Evolution: an Illustrated Introduction, Roger Lewin, C. 1984, W.H. Freeman and Company, N.Y., p. 59, for an example of a situation where plant matter was believed to have been present yet has produced no fossil evidence.

[46]See The Cambridge Encyclopedia of Earth Sciences, Ed. David G. Smith Ph.D., C. 1981, Crown Publishers Inc. / Cambridge University Press, N.Y., p. 325.

[47]See The Panda's Thumb, S.J. Gould, C. 1980, W.W. Norton & Co., N.Y., p. 219.

[48]See The Cambridge Encyclopedia of Earth Sciences, Ed. David G. Smith Ph.D., C. 1981, Crown Publishers Inc. / Cambridge University Press, N.Y., pp. 261, 262.

the dry land while the first aquatic animals were appearing. One source describes the land as "A barren, lifeless desert."[49] Another source says, "The initial 'greening' of the landscape by green algae and bacteria may have taken place at or before this time." (Here "this time" appears to refer to when oxygen first became abundant – long before the first aquatic animals.)[50] As explained in the previous chapter, we should be skeptical in those cases where witnesses disagree; contradicting testimony is *not* adequately founded upon truth. The opinions of the scientists will, therefore, be disregarded here until they have found evidence on which to ground their claims.

About two billion years ago (after the continents had formed but before the first evidence of multicelled aquatic animals), there was a significant change in the composition of the earth's atmosphere. Evidence from iron oxide in mineral deposits indicates that this is when it first began containing large amounts of oxygen.[51] It is commonly assumed by scientists that this oxygen was produced by the blue-green algae which had lived in the earth's shallow seas almost since those seas were formed – that at this time, the algae finally started making headway against the processes which were removing oxygen from the atmosphere. But whether or not the first land plants had appeared by this time to help them out is not really a scientifically settled question.

In the past, the Bible has had a record of being correct (even if misunderstood) when scientific knowledge was wrong or incomplete. Because of this, and because the Bible seems to provide no justification for an alternate interpretation, it is

---

[49]Our Changing Planet, John Gribbin, C. 1977, Thomas Y. Crowell Company, N.Y., p. 12.

[50]See The Cambridge Encyclopedia of Earth Sciences, Ed. David G. Smith Ph.D., C. 1981, Crown Publishers Inc. / Cambridge University Press, N.Y., p. 374. Oxygen atoms are released by plants – aquatic or otherwise.

[51]See Origins: a Skeptic's Guide to the Creation of Life on Earth, Robert Shapiro, C. 1986, Summit Books, N.Y., pp. 92, 93. When oxygen is present, ozone forms in the upper atmosphere. It is normally assumed that until this ozone layer formed – protecting the bare land from the sun's harmful ultra-violet radiation – that more complex plants and animals could not safely live on the land; but if this author's understanding of the fourth day is correct, then there probably would have been sufficient water vapor present in the atmosphere to protect the early terrestrial plants.

probably the scientific evidence that is lacking here. As will be seen, it is unreasonable to exclude the Cambrian "explosion" of aquatic life from whatever God might have meant by having the waters "teem with living creatures" — the fifth day. There must have been some form of plant life living on the dry land preceding the Cambrian period. Scientists are unjustified in claiming the absence of Precambrian terrestrial plant life on such poor authority as the absence of evidence which is not expected to be very likely in any case. It is possible that this evidence might still be discovered some time in the future. Perhaps more digging (literally) on the part of the scientists will turn up some actual terrestrial fossils from the time period in question. Meanwhile we must just be patient and wait.

Another interesting point is that the Bible says the plants, as well as all the other created life forms, were created to reproduce "according to their kinds."[52] This statement is not in agreement with Darwin's theory of gradual and continuous evolution; but the fossil record has stubbornly borne out Genesis and not Darwin in this regard. New "kinds" of life just seem to appear, and then remain essentially unchanged for their entire stay on the planet. This has been, in many cases, a great many millions of years![53] Here the traditional understanding of the Bible has stood firmly where the most popular scientific *theory* has needed continuous readjustment.

---

[52]What exactly "kind" (Hebrew "miyn") means is not clearly distinguished by ancient Hebrew. The word could mean form, species, kind, or sort. Gesenius' Hebrew-Chaldee Lexicon to the Old Testament, C. 1979, Baker Book House, Michigan, p. 470, (entry #4327). The biologists have not been much help either as their definitions are not very firm — and usually based on evolutionary assumptions. This author has some very specific opinions about this and may explain them in another book.

[53]The Panda's Thumb, Stephen Jay Gould, C. 1980, W.W. Norton & Co., N.Y., pp. 182-184.

Day 4: The Great Lights
Genesis 1:14-19

"And God said, 'Let there be lights in the expanse of the sky to separate the day from the night, and let them serve as signs to mark seasons and days and years, and let them be lights in the expanse of the sky to give light on the earth.' And it was so. God made two great lights – the greater light to govern the day and the lesser light to govern the night. He also made the stars. God set them in the expanse of the sky to give light on the earth, to govern the day and the night, and to separate light from darkness. And God saw that it was good. And there was evening, and there was morning – the fourth day."

This presents another apparent difficulty; according to the traditional interpretation, the sun is being "made" again. The scientists assure us that the sun was burning brightly long before there were any plants upon the earth; the Bible tells us that light preceded vegetation. We must agree with both. Plants *do* need light to grow. Furthermore, because light can be seen from very distant stars – light which has been in transit even longer than our sun has been around – there must have been plenty of stars back then too. Although theories concerning the formation of the moon are still being developed, the evidence shows that the moon was also created long before this time.

Another complication is that it appears that God is telling us that He "set" the sun, moon and stars in the "expanse" (the space between the waters) rather than in outer space where they certainly are. (Of course the word that meant the "expanse" between the waters could also refer to the "expanse" of outer space. Words do have multiple meanings.)

It seems another understanding of verses 14-19 is necessary – either this, or else another understanding of Genesis 1:3 and of all the scientific evidence as well. Something did happen at about this time which may provide an explanation.

Back during the second day, the waters were divided into liquid water below and very thick dark clouds above. At that time, a hypothetical observer standing on the surface of the earth (perhaps in a boat[54]) would have no way of knowing that there were stars or even a sun; the clouds would have been too thick. He would know about day and night but would have no way of knowing that the brighter sky of the day was illuminated from behind by the sun. He would not be able to observe how the sun's arc across the sky would be higher in the summer than in the winter. He would not be able to observe the summer stars as they replaced the winter ones and then were, in turn, replaced themselves. In other words, he would not have the sun, moon and stars to tell him of the days, seasons, and years. He would have the continuing cycle of light and darkness;[55] but that would be all.

What appears to have happened on the fourth day is that God caused the cloud cover to thin and finally to break up. At this point, it would seem to our earthbound observer (who by now has some land to stand on) that the sun and stars had just come into being. Furthermore they would appear to him to be in the sky rather than in outer space – of which he knows nothing. To him, it would appear as if they had not existed at all until that moment. From that time on, they would be visible for him to use for reckoning days, seasons and years – but not before. This would put this verse in the class of verses called "observer true" – like those verses which say "the sun rose," when in fact the sun stayed where it was as the earth turned toward it.

This meaning – first presentation of the formerly hidden sun etc. – is compatible with the words which God used. There are only two words from which the difficulty actually arises, "made" used in "God *made* two great lights" and "set" used in "God *set* them in the expanse of the sky." "Made" is translated from the Hebrew "asah" and "set" from the Hebrew "nathan." Where our English translations say "he also made the stars," the Hebrew

---

[54]This boat would have to be chiseled out of solid rock as there were no trees yet. Also the observer would need to carry his own oxygen supply, etc.

[55]At that time a day-night cycle would have lasted considerably less than 24 hours. The earth's rotation has slowed down since then. See The Panda's Thumb, by Stephen Jay Gould, C. 1980, W.W. Norton and Company, N.Y., pp. 316, 319.

merely says "also the stars."[56] Other than the way these words have been translated, there is no problem with this passage referring to the breaking up of the clouds.[57] Each of these words will be examined here.[58]

"Asah," the Hebrew for "made," is a different word than the one used back in the first verse where God "created" the heaven and the earth. There the word was "bara" which, as was explained, means "to carve out." The meaning of "Asah" is more general. It can mean "to labor," "to work about (or upon) anything," "to make," or "to produce by labor."[59] The word is translated many different ways. Some Biblical examples (K.J.V.) are: to *deal* kindly (Gen. 24:49), to *work* in gold (Exodus 31:4), to *commit* a sin (Lev. 5:17), to *prepare* bread (Gen. 27:17), or even to *show* kindness (Gen. 24:12).[60]

The King James Version of the Bible translated "asah" as "do" more than it translated it any other way, more than twice as many times as it translated it "make" – which was the second most common rendering. Still the most precise[61] translation would be more like to "prepare" or "produce." These carry more of the actual color of "asah" than the nondescript "do." It would be more accurate to say that a cow *produces* milk than that a cow *does* milk (asah is translated "gives milk" in Isaiah 7:22).

---

[56]See The NIV Interlinear Hebrew-English Old Testament, Vol. 1, Ed. John R. Kohlenberger III, C. 1979, Zondervan Publishing House, Grand Rapids, Michigan, p. 2, Verse 16.

[57]Some creationists would disagree with this based on their theories concerning Noah's flood. Of course theological theories are not the same thing as scriptural truth. Here we need only concern ourselves that we are in agreement with the Bible's actual words.

[58]Another possibility to consider is that "made" could be translated "had made" (as it sometimes is, such as in Genesis 2:8, 9). See The Genesis Debate, Ronald Youngblood, C. 1986, Thomas Nelson Publishers, Nashville, p. 38, the "no" argument; pp. 45-46, the "yes" argument.

[59]Gesenius' Hebrew-Chaldee Lexicon to the Old Testament, C. 1979, Baker Book House, Michigan, pp. 657, 658, (entry #6213).

[60]The Hebrew examples and statistics used in this chapter are based on the K.J.V. and are from Young's Concordance to the Bible, Robert Young LL.D., C. 1964, William B. Eerdmans Publishing Company, Grand Rapids, Michigan.

[61]Here the term "most precise" is used instead of the translator's technical term "most literal" to avoid confusion with the other sense of the term "literal" (as opposed to spiritual, figurative, or symbolic). By the term "most literal" a translator merely means the most exact or most common translation.

The most exact translation might go something like, "And God *produced* two of the great lights."[62] This tells us nothing about how they got there. The translation that God *made* two great lights actually adds a shade of meaning (something like "built") which the Hebrew doesn't necessarily carry. Another translator could, just as properly, have added a different shade of meaning such as "worked on;" this would be as close to "asah" as "make" is. "Bring forth" is even an acceptable translation for the word (Lev. 25:21). It would seem that "asah" is a versatile enough word that it would fit properly almost regardless of how God caused the sun, moon and stars to appear in the sky.

Next, the word "set," translated from the Hebrew "nathan," will be examined. Like "asah," "nathan" is also translated in a wealth of different ways – for example to *deliver* them, (Gen. 32:16) to *bring* a snare, (Proverbs. 29:25) *put* out his hand, (Gen. 38:28) or *make* a covenant (Gen. 17:2). The most common translation of "nathan" is "give."[63] The King James Version translates "nathan" as "give" more than five times as often as it translates it any other way.

Instead of "God *set* them in the expanse of the sky," the Hebrew merely says, "God *gave* them in the expanse ..." "Set" carries the idea of a relocation – one which is not necessarily implied by "nathan." Here it would improve the English grammar without altering the Hebrew meaning to use a synonym of "gave" and say that God "presented" them (Ezek. 20:28). This verse can be translated so the sky assumes the sense of a display window through which the presentation is made rather than the location where the great lights would be placed; this interpretation removes any problem of apparent misplacement.

"Nathan," like "asah," will fit with almost any theory a person cares to propose. Again we seem to have a rather versatile word.

If the Bible had been translated to allow for modern scientific information, Genesis 1:14-18 might read:

---

[62]The Hebrew says, "two *of the* great lights." See The NIV Interlinear Hebrew-English Old Testament, Vol. 1, Ed. John R. Kohlenberger III, C. 1979, Zondervan Publishing House, Grand Rapids, Michigan, p. 2, Verse 16.

[63]Gesenius' Hebrew-Chaldee Lexicon to the Old Testament, C. 1979, Baker Book House, Michigan, pp. 572-574, (entry #5414).

And God said, "Let there be lights in the expanse of the sky to separate between day and night. Let them be as signs for seasons and days and years. And let them be for lights in the expanse of the sky to give light to the earth." And it was so. And God produced two of the great lights – the greater light to rule the day and the lesser to rule the night, then also the stars. God presented them in the expanse of the sky to light the earth and to govern over the day and the night and to separate between light and darkness. And God saw that it was good.[64]

This is closer to the original Hebrew than most English translations are. A slightly more scientifically biased rendering, although as accurate as other English translations, could have replaced "produced" with "brought forth." This would be more consistent with previously created astronomical objects being revealed by the removal of a thick cloud cover.

Notice also that the order of appearance further confirms the idea that these lights became increasingly visible through a decreasing cloud cover. The order of appearance begins with those which are the most easily seen through the clouds and proceeds to those which are least easily seen. First the sun, next the moon and finally the stars would become visible.

Of course, God's use of such versatile words as "asah" and "nathan" does not prove that He did not actually fabricate the sun, moon and stars right then; those words could be taken either way. But they do allow harmony between the fourth-day description and what is known to be the truth from other evidence: The Bible says there was light back in verse three; there is good scientific evidence that this light came from the sun. Because this is not changing the meaning of any of the original Hebrew words, it is justifiable that this verse be interpreted in a nontraditional manner; when the scientific data is taken into consideration, there is more total information available than most translators have.

---

[64]This was modeled after <u>The NIV Interlinear Hebrew-English Old Testament Vol. 1</u>, Ed. John R. Kohlenberger III, C. 1979, Zondervan Publishing House, Grand Rapids, Michigan, p. 2.

Day 5: Fish and Birds

Genesis 1:20-23

"And God said, 'Let the water teem with living creatures, and let birds fly above the earth across the expanse of the sky.' So God created the great creatures of the sea and every living and moving thing with which the water teems, according to their kinds, and every winged bird according to its kind. And God saw that it was good. God blessed them and said, 'Be fruitful and increase in number and fill the water in the seas, and let the birds increase on the earth.' And there was evening, and there was morning – the fifth day."

Here, the Bible says God created aquatic creatures and birds – probably in the order mentioned. The scientists are a little more specific: The first known multicelled aquatic animal life appeared five or six hundred million years ago. True fishes first appeared a little later – about four hundred million years ago.[65]

There were some specific moments during earth's history when many species appeared within a very short period. The creation of aquatic animals was probably the most remarkable of these moments. Scientists call this event the "Cambrian explosion." The term "explosion" was appropriately selected because of the appearance of almost every imaginable form of aquatic life (with the single exception of those with backbones – true fish for example) within a very short period of time.[66] This is an interesting companion to the Bible's phrase "Let the water teem with living creatures." The two almost certainly refer to the same event. Notice this match confirms the very nature of this appearance as well as the mere fact of it. Here is another

---

[65]For comparison, blue-green algae, which is the earliest known plant-like life form and which is also aquatic, has been around since about 3.5 billion years ago. The first land plants may have been created one or two billion years ago, although there is presently no evidence for them.

[66]See "The Emergence of Animals," by Mark A.S. McMenamin, SCIENTIFIC AMERICAN, April 1987, Vol. 256, No. 4, pp. 94+.

impressive match between the old-earth understanding of Genesis and the scientific evidence.

True feathered birds – although having teeth – first appeared with the dinosaurs about 150 million years ago. This date is perhaps a little shaky. In order to fly, birds must have light-weight bones. Hence they do not fossilize very well. (Birds fossilize better than plants do, however.) The oldest birds known to scientists might not be the very oldest ones there were.

Interestingly, the word "bird" may also be introducing some confusion. "Bird" is translated from the Hebrew "owph" which means merely "a wing."[67] It also carries the idea of "wing covered."[68] This is not necessarily a bird. In Leviticus, for example, this word is used in conjunction with a grasshopper!

> "There are, however, some *winged* creatures that walk on all fours that you may eat;"
>
> – Leviticus 11:21, Emphasis mine.

(Emphasized word translated from the Hebrew "owph.")

Even though grasshoppers are not "birds," as we understand the term, they are still included in the Biblical category of "owph." In this same chapter of Leviticus, "owph" is also used in reference to a bat (compare verses 13 and 19). We must keep reminding ourselves that Genesis, like Leviticus, was written a long time ago; we should not be surprised if we have to temporarily lay aside our twentieth-century understanding of animal classifications if we are to interpret it correctly. Genesis was written in ancient Hebrew, not in modern technical English.

It would seem that God may include flying insects in with this category too – or possibly even all "bugs."[69] This pushes the date for the first appearance of "owph" back to about 350

---

[67]Gesenius' Hebrew-Chaldee Lexicon to the Old Testament, C. 1979, Baker Book House, Michigan, p. 614, (entry #5775).

[68]The Hebrew-Chaldee Lexicon to Strong's Exhaustive Concordance of the Bible, James Strong S.T.D., LL.D., Riverside Book and Bible House, Iowa Falls, Iowa 50126. (Entry #5775.)

[69]Scorpions, for example, appear in the fossil record before winged insects.

million years ago[70] – farther back than any other exclusively land dwelling animal including the dinosaurs. This is still after the first aquatic animals. It is about the time of the first amphibians.

Day 6: Animals and Men

Genesis 1:24, 25

"And God said, 'Let the land produce living creatures according to their kinds: livestock, creatures that move along the ground, and wild animals, each according to its kind.' And it was so. God made the wild animals according to their kinds, the livestock according to their kinds, and all the creatures that move along the ground according to their kinds. And God saw that it was good.

These two verses primarily refer to mammals – most of which have appeared only within the last sixty-five million years. The oldest dinosaurs date from roughly 230 million years ago. Because dinosaurs did "move" along the ground and were "wild animals," it seems reasonable to include them here. That would make this category older than the oldest known true birds. Therefore, if we were to disallow bugs from the bird category, this would cause a chronological problem.

This discrepancy might just reflect an unfortunate lack of bird fossils; as has been explained, the fossil evidence for birds is not as complete as that for the dinosaurs. However, a lack of fossils is probably not what is happening here; it seems that God may include winged insects – and possibly *all* "bugs" – in with His group "birds." According to the fossils, "bugs" appeared before any other land animals. This would completely eliminate the chronological problem. It is not at all a conventional approach; but it is a possible way to solve the problem without abandoning the scientific or scriptural evidence.

---

[70]Cockroaches are among the oldest winged insects – appearing 350 million years ago. (They can and do occasionally fly!) See, The Audubon Society Field Guide to North American Insects and Spiders, Lorus and Margery Milne, C. 1980, Alfred A. Knopf Inc., N.Y., p. 391.

Genesis 1:26, 27

"Then God said, 'Let us make man in our image, in our likeness, and let them rule over the fish of the sea and the birds of the air, over the livestock, over all the earth, and over all the creatures that move along the ground.' So God created man in his own image ..."

This brings us up to God's last creation; man is the final entry in the list which Genesis 1 supplies. The oldest creature that anyone ever dares to call a man, Homo habilis, appeared about two or three million years ago.[71] Even though Homo habilis made and used tools (sharp flakes which he chipped off of rocks), he was not really a man.[72] In fact, he was *quite unlike* modern man.

There are also some more recent man-like creatures: Homo erectus, Homo sapiens neanderthalensis, and Archaic homo. Homo erectus first appeared about 1.5 million years ago[73] and Homo sapiens neanderthalensis about 150 thousand years ago.[74] This last date falls in the dating gap. As explained in the previous chapter, it is difficult to date fossils from this period; so this date should be treated with some caution. Archaic homo is a loosely defined category which is sometimes applied to Homo erectus and sometimes to another species of man-like ape which seems to be coming into focus in the fossil record. This new creature is presently thought to fill the gap between Homo erectus and true moderns; this gap was once supposed to have been bridged by the Neanderthals. Archaic homo (the new creature) has sometimes been classified as a Neanderthal[75] and

---

[71]This particular date has been one of the most hotly contested potassium-argon dates ever. Still the most wildly variant dates fall more or less within the 2-3 million year age range. Lucy: the Beginnings of Humankind, Donald C. Johanson and Maitland A. Edey, C. 1981, Warner Books, N.Y., pp. 238-243.

[72]Some creationists consider Homo habilis to be a man, however.

[73]Ascent to Civilization, John Gowlett, C. 1984, Alfred A. Knopf Inc., N.Y., p. 60.

[74]Ibid p. 104.

[75]Atlas of Ancient Archaeology, Jacquetta Hawkes, C. 1974, McGraw-Hill Book Company, N.Y., p. 197.

sometimes as a modern.[76] All of these other creatures should be excluded from the category of true men; even though they looked more like men and made more advanced tools than Homo habilis did, they still were not men.

Although theologians often insist there could never have been any man-like ape creatures, this is merely a theological theory based on our understanding of the Biblical phrase "after their kinds." The Bible does not actually tell us God didn't create them; whereas the fossil evidence tells us He did. There are obvious similarities between the man-like apes and modern man; but this does *not* prove we evolved from them. Because we believe God's creatures breed true to their "kinds," those man-like creatures must have been separate creations of God – similar to us, but also different. Denying their existence is a step away from God's truth – not toward it.

Although we may be uncomfortable with the idea of a nonhuman creature who made and used tools, we have no scriptural reason to be. We may wonder *why* God created them;[77] but we have no scriptural grounds to insist He didn't. Their existence may damage the pride we take in our "lofty" status as humans; but God has never promised us that we had anything to be proud of anyway (Psalm 103:14) – only that we would rule over His creation (Genesis 1:28). We might like to be the only intelligent creatures God ever created but we are not. The brain design of Neanderthal man was indeed remarkable;[78] and so is that of a modern bottle-nosed dolphin. In fact, a dolphin's brain is larger than a modern man's is. Dolphins are

---

[76]Ascent to Civilization, John Gowlett, C. 1984, Alfred A. Knopf Inc., N.Y., p. 118.

[77]This author has some definite opinions on this subject which may be explained in a later book. There is some fascinating scriptural evidence which might have led us to expect God's creation of these man-like apes if we had only been keeping our eyes open!

[78]Sources disagree as to whether the size of the Neanderthal's brain was, on the average, larger or smaller than modern man's. According to Prehistoric Man: the Fascinating Story of Man's Evolution, John Waechter, C. 1977, Octopus Books Limited, London, p. 60, their average brain size was 300 cc. smaller than ours and was much less developed in terms of surface area. A more recent source, Human Evolution: an Illustrated Introduction, Roger Lewin, C. 1984, W.H. Freeman Co., N.Y., pp. 72, 73, claims that the Neanderthals had slightly larger (by about 40 cc.) brains than ours; here the "extra" capacity is thought to be for control of their extra muscles.

very intelligent creatures and God certainly made them. We have to admit we share this planet with other intelligent creatures! It could be argued that the biggest advantage we have over dolphins is not our brains but our hands.[79]

Never the less, *Adam was created in God's image while those other creatures were not.* To sharpen the division between us and them, there is no physical evidence that any of them ever wore clothes – not even for warmth. Although the claim is often made that the Neanderthals wore clothes, there is no supporting evidence; It is merely assumed that they did because they lived in cold climates.[80] It is not known for sure that they didn't have sufficient body hair for warmth.[81] The first actual evidence of clothing and of bone sewing needles does not appear until fully modern man does.[82] This evidence indicates that the knowledge of sin (and therefore Adam's fall) came with modern man. This is another reason those earlier creatures should not be considered true men.

Many other traits which are normally considered human did not appear until fully modern man either. The earliest undisputed art first appears at the same time as the moderns do.[83] Although it was recently believed that Neanderthals buried their dead, this idea has now been brought under question.[84] The earliest

---

[79] Of course this statement is extremely anthropocentric (viewed only in terms of human values). A porpoise might not regard our hand as sufficient compensation for our lack of sonar related abilities.

[80] The Making of Mankind, Richard E. Leakey, C. 1981, E.P. Dutton, N.Y., p. 150. This source makes the assumption of clothing based on the cold habitat. See also Prehistoric Man: the Fascinating Story of Man's Evolution, John Waechter, C. 1977, Octopus Books Limited, London, p. 57. for the same reasoning.

[81] Human Evolution: an Illustrated Introduction, by Roger Lewin, C. 1984, W.H. Freeman and Company, N.Y., p. 53. This source says that it is not known when the short, fine hair of modern humans appeared.

[82] Ascent to Civilization, John Gowlett, C. 1984, Alfred A. Knopf Inc., N.Y., p. 123. See for earliest known sewing tools. See also Prehistoric Man: the Fascinating Story of Man's Evolution, John Waechter, C. 1977, Octopus Books Limited, London, pp. 63, 65. The first evidence of clothing was only preserved by ornamental beads.

[83] Ascent to Civilization, John Gowlett, C. 1984, Alfred A. Knopf Inc., N.Y., p. 128.

[84] "Grave Doubts, The Neanderthals may not have buried their dead after all," John Benditt, SCIENTIFIC AMERICAN, June 1989, Vol. 260, No. 6, pp. 32, 33.

presently-undisputed burials appear at the same time as modern man does. The fossil evidence also indicates that articulate speech was not possible for the Neanderthals. Their vocal tract did not have the right shape.[85]

God made Adam a fully modern man (Homo sapiens sapiens). Exactly how long ago modern man appeared is hard to say. History only provides recent dates – from within the last 7000 years. It is certain that man was around before then – probably *long* before then; it is just difficult to know how much before.

Unfortunately, radioactive dating techniques are of only limited help here. The event was too recent for the potassium-argon method to do any good, and it is too long ago to be accurately pinpointed by carbon-14. According to most sources, the oldest fossils of modern man date by carbon-14 to around thirty-five or forty thousand years ago; but this date is rather shaky. As explained in the previous chapter, carbon-14 needs calibration and the calibration has, so far, only been worked out to about nine thousand years ago.

Some remains identified as "fully modern humans," have been found which date (using exotic methods) as early as about a hundred thousand years old.[86] These fossils are considered modern men although some of them are said to display some "primitive features." Unfortunately, the term "modern man" is sometimes loosely used to cover both the true moderns and the archaics. Are these fossils truly modern men? Are they really Archaic homo? Are there some of each represented? Or is something else entirely different going on?

---

[85]"Hard Words," Philip E. Ross, SCIENTIFIC AMERICAN, April 1991, Vol. 264, No. 4, p. 147.

[86]"ESR dates for the hominid burial site of Qafzeh in Israel," H. P Schwarcz et al. JOURNAL OF HUMAN EVOLUTION, December 1988, Vol. 17, No. 8, pp. 733-734. See also "Visual Thinking in the Ice Age," Randall White, SCIENTIFIC AMERICAN, July 1989, Vol. 261, No. 1, p. 92. There are also genetic arguments which place the age of modern man somewhere in the 50-250 thousand-year range. Genetic arguments are based on mathematical analysis of the mitochondrial DNA of living people. Such arguments are not yet considered very reliable. If an intelligent creator has been methodically modifying DNA, perhaps in *several* female individuals for each new species (Eve, Cain's wife ...), then the method encounters an unexpected difficulty which makes it nearly useless.

Although questions concerning the man-like apes might keep both scientists and theologians up nights, they really aren't that important to us right here; for the present purposes, it is only important that man fits into his proper place in the chronological order of God's creation. This has been properly established. The conventional date of thirty-five to forty thousand years will be assumed for this event, although it could be *substantially* in error.

Back in 1650 AD, James Ussher,[87] the Archbishop of Armagh, attempted to calculate the year in which God created Adam by using the genealogies provided in the Bible. He came up with a date of 4004 BC.[88] This is about 6000 years ago. It does *not* agree with the scientific evidence which we have just examined. The reason for this becomes apparent when we take a closer look at the Biblical genealogies.

It can be seen from comparing the genealogies from Genesis with the ones given in Luke[89] that the Biblical lists are not as complete as we would like them to be. Luke 3:35, 36, for example, records a second Cainan between Arphaxad and Sala (also spelled Shelah or Salah) which is not found in the parallel genealogy of Genesis 11:12. This is a warning that we can't be certain the type of calculation Ussher performed will give us meaningful dates.

Because of this, even young-earth creationists do not hold rigidly to the 6000-year age. Most of them assume about ten thousand years ago for the date of the creation of the earth – and therefore of Adam as well. (Remember that they consider Adam to have been created within a mere 144 hours of the time the heavens and Earth were created.) For example:

"Furthermore, the genealogies listed in Genesis and elsewhere in the Bible, it is believed, would restrict the

---

[87]"Ussher" is also correctly spelled "Usher."

[88]Appendix 5 has been included for anyone who is interested in an attempted reconstruction of Ussher's calculations.

[89]Luke's genealogies follow those listed in the Septuagint, the Greek translation of the Hebrew scriptures which was commonly used during his day.

time of creation to somewhere between six thousand and about ten thousand years ago."

Evolution: the Fossils Say No!, by Duane T. Gish, Ph.D., C. 1979, Creation-Life Publishers, San Diego, California, p. 60.

"To the extent that *sound* archaeological research may *require* dating of early human settlements at dates earlier than the traditional Ussher chronology allows, the Bible does indicate the possibility of minor gaps in the genealogies..."

Scientific Creationism, edited by Henry M. Morris, Ph.D., C. 1974, Master Books, El Cajon, California, p. 250, Emphasis theirs.

The point here is that even those who hold most rigidly to the traditional interpretation of the Biblical text do not regard Ussher's type of computing to be a reliable method of interpreting the Bible. Because there are well-founded historic dates which force human history back farther than these calculations allow,[90] and because of the known existence of some gaps in the genealogies, it might be more reasonable (within some sort of limits) to assume that the historic and archaeological dates are approximately correct.

The authors of Scientific Creationism (pp. 247-250), quite reasonably, explain that they are reluctant to allow for gaps accounting for the million years which they regard as the evolutionist's measure of human history; but *we are not evolutionists* and are not claiming Adam was a pre-human man-like ape creature (such as a Neanderthal). We need only account for the age of modern man.

---

[90]For example, according to Egyptologist James Henry Breasted, the Egyptians invented the 365 day calendar in the year 4236 B.C. See The Conquest of Civilization, James Henry Breasted, C. 1926, 1938, The Literary Guild of America, Inc., N.Y., p. 56. This date is not directly tied to historic records but was calculated relative to an astronomical observation concerning a more recent, but purportedly mathematically related, event. Also ancient Chinese family's genealogies pre-date Ussher's creation date. See Continents in Collision, by Russell Miller, C. 1983, Time-Life Books, Alexandria, Virginia, p. 10.

Even so, the thirty-five or forty thousand years conservatively assumed for modern man would constitute a lot of gaps. If modern man turns out to be older than this, then there are even more gaps to account for. The young-earth creationists seem to be thinking more on the order of merely a few thousand extra years. Gish, for example, has allowed for about four thousand extra years. Because there is no scriptural evidence which limits these gaps to what the young-earth creationists are recommending, it will be assumed here that there are a great many gaps;[91] that they can account for this discrepancy.

The scientific dating might be somewhat in error, but this won't completely remove the problem. Carbon-14 can be calibrated back about nine thousand years (although not yet 40,000 years) and it has been found that, if anything, the carbon-14 dates are actually too young – *not* too old (see Chapter 5). Anyway, there are other kinds of evidence which tend to confirm the carbon-14 dates. Other dating techniques are more suspect, but we should not *just assume* they are wrong if we have learned anything at all from this book. It is quite likely that the error lies in *our traditional understanding* of scripture.[92]

Although we may not be comfortable with this many gaps, we have no evidence that the truth should be what we are most comfortable with. Truth can sometimes be hard to hear. Maybe some future advance in the scientific understanding of early man will suddenly throw light on all of the presently obscure Biblical passages and clear this all up. Perhaps the solution will come directly through advances in Biblical understanding. Meanwhile we will have to be patient. It is at times like this that keeping one's mind open is the recommended course of action.

---

[91]The Bible sometimes provides extremely abridged genealogies – for example Matthew 1:1, "Jesus Christ, the son of David, the son of Abraham."

[92]It has also been suggested that God might have created other men who lived long ago but who were not Adam's descendants. See God is Light, Foster H. Shannon, C. 1981, Green Leaf Press, P.O. Box 5, Campbell, Ca. 95008, p. 51. The Bible calls Adam the first man (1 Corinthians 15:45) but it also calls Jesus the "Last Adam." This tends to imply that something else besides "the absolute first man" may have been intended. If this is true, we must still consider the fact that some of those other men wore clothes. This would separate them from the other ape-like creatures; it would seem that they must also have had a knowledge of sin. Perhaps something like this is what the very obscure mention of "the sons of God" in Genesis 6:2 referres to; but this is just wild speculation.

Conclusions

The scientific evidence has not been as hard on Genesis 1 as we might have expected. It has been necessary to make a few adjustments to our **traditional understanding**, but it has *not* been necessary to abandon either **scriptural authority** or **scientific evidence**. Cautious interpretation can produce a very remarkable fit − a fit which not only matches the coarse data but some very fine points as well. Instead of opposing the Bible, scientific evidence elaborates upon it and helps us to choose between the different possible interpretations.

God's creation can be used as a powerful commentary on what Genesis really means. Remember, God "wrote" both accounts. What better source is there to consult about what a book means than another book by that very same author − especially one which covers the same information? Of course there is always that author Himself. Readers are encouraged, as they check the scriptures to see if this information is correct (and the libraries), to seek God and ask for His help. His word would be true even if every man were found to be a liar! (Romans 3:4).

Once again, the reader is reminded that none of the statements in this chapter are dogmatic claims. It is not known for certain which meaning or meanings God actually intended in the Scriptures. The possibilities which have been proposed merely appear to be in harmony with both God's written Word and His created universe as we understand them at the present time. Whether or not this understanding is truth, time will judge. Knowledge will increase and when it does, remaining errors will be exposed. We must continue to test everything; and we must hold on to the good. Furthermore, we must avoid those things which prove to be false (1 Thess. 5:21, 22).

Summary of Genesis Chapter One

Here the various statements made in this chapter will be summarized. The statements are arranged alongside the N.I.V. Biblical text to expedite comparison. Grouping is both by scriptural "day" and scientific age.

Day 1:   **About 15-20 billion years ago**

Genesis 1:1

"In the beginning God created the heavens and the earth."

God created matter, space and time.

About 4.5 billion years ago

Genesis 1:2

"Now the earth was formless and empty, darkness was over the surface of the deep, and the Spirit of God was hovering over the waters."

The matter from which God formed our earth and solar system comprised a shapeless nebula in dark space. God set to work on it to accomplish His intentions.

About 4.5 billion years ago

Genesis 1:3

"And God said, 'Let there be light,' and there was light."

Sunlight became visible from earth at this time. At some point, God caused the sun to ignite — quite literally as a giant continuously-burning hydrogen bomb. This verse may either refer to this or to when God cleared some of the nebular dust away.

Genesis 1:4, 5

"God saw that the light was good, and he separated the light from the darkness. God called the light 'day,' and the darkness he called 'night.' And there was evening, and there was morning — the first day."

God finished clearing the nebular dust away and the earth cooled. The earth's back side became dark. Its original atmosphere was stripped.

Day 2:

About 4 billion years ago

Genesis 1:6-8

"And God said, 'Let there be an expanse between the waters to separate water from water.' So God made the expanse and separated the water under the expanse from the water above it. And it was so. God called the expanse 'sky.' And there was evening, and there was morning — the second day."

The earth cooled some more. Some of the volcanic steam which now surrounded it condensed into water which covered the earth's surface. God made an air space between the dark clouds and the surface water.

Day 3:

About 2.5-3 billion years ago

Genesis 1:9, 10

"And God said, 'Let the water under the sky be gathered to one place, and let dry ground appear.' And it was so. God called the dry ground 'land,' and the gathered waters he called 'seas.' And God saw that it was good.''

God caused the earth's crust to form continents which pushed up through the oceans. (God had created single-celled plant-like aquatic life by this time.)

Date undetermined – maybe 1-2 billion years ago

Genesis 1:11-13

"Then God said, 'Let the land produce vegetation: seed-bearing plants and trees on the land that bear fruit with seed in it, according to their various kinds.' And it was so. The land produced vegetation: plants bearing seed according to their kinds and trees bearing fruit with seed in it according to their kinds. And God saw that it was good. And there was evening, and there was morning – the third day.''

The first terrestrial plants must have been created at this time. There is, as yet, no fossil evidence for them. Large amounts of oxygen first appeared in the atmosphere about 2 billion years ago. God continued to create other kinds of plants during subsequent "days."

Day 4:

Genesis 1:14-19

"And God said, 'Let there be lights in the expanse of the sky to separate the day from the night, and let them serve as signs to mark seasons and days and years, and let them be lights in the expanse of the sky to give light on the earth.' And it was so. God made two great lights – the greater light to govern the day and the lesser light to govern the night. He also made the stars. God set them in the expanse of the sky to give light on the earth, to govern the day and the night, and to separate light from darkness. And God saw that it was good. And there was evening, and there was morning – the fourth day."

God "brought forth" the sun, moon and stars in that order by clearing the thick cloud layer from around the earth. He "presented" them in the heavens where they could be used for the figuring of seasons etc.

Day 5   **About 500-600 million years ago**

Genesis 1:20-23

"And God said, 'Let the water teem with living creatures, and let birds fly above the earth across the expanse of the sky.' So God created the great creatures of the sea and every living and moving thing with which the water teems, according to their kinds, and every winged bird according to its kind. And God saw that it was good. God blessed them and said, 'Be fruitful and increase in number and fill the water in the seas, and let the birds increase on the earth.' And there was evening, and there was morning – the fifth day."

God created an "explosion" of aquatic life forms. He began making true fish a little later – 400 million years ago. The first "winged creatures" were insects – 350 million years ago. God made the first amphibians 350-300 million years ago. The oldest known true feathered birds appear overlapping day six – during the time of the dinosaurs.

Day 6:   **About 230 million years ago**

Genesis 1:24, 25

"And God said, 'Let the land produce living creatures according to their kinds: livestock, creatures that move along the ground, and wild animals, each according to its kind.' And it was so. God made the wild animals according to their kinds, the livestock according to their kinds, and all the creatures that move along the ground according to their kinds. And God saw that it was good."

God made the reptiles, including the dinosaurs, beginning about 230 million years ago. Most mammals were created later – beginning 65 million years ago. God created the first tool-using man-like apes about 2-3 million years ago.

Possibly 40 thousand years ago

Genesis 1:26, 27

"Then God said, 'Let us make man in our image, in our likeness, and let them rule over the fish of the sea and the birds of the air, over the livestock, over all the earth, and over all the creatures that move along the ground.' So God created man in his own image ..."

God created Adam – the first fully modern man.

Chapter 7:
Repairing the Damage

"Always be prepared to give an answer to everyone who asks you to give the reason for the hope that you have. **But do this with gentleness and respect**."
                                    – 1 Peter 3:15, Emphasis mine.

As explained at the beginning of this book, before we attempt to correct atheists, we have been instructed to remove errors from our own arguments (Matthew 7:5). Consequently, the church must abandon the young-earth position. This applies to *all* of us – not just the relatively small number of vocal creationists who are promoting the young-earth error in their lectures and books. Leaders without followers are not really leaders at all. Therefore we are *all* responsible and must all do what we can to correct the error.

Probably the most important first step which we need to take is to stop laughing when an atheist is made out to be a fool by a Christian. Laughing in this sense is a way of showing someone that we have judged them to be a fool. "The fool says in his heart, 'there is no God.'" (Psalm 14:1). But we should never laugh – not even at true fools. In Matthew, Jesus warns us:

> "Do not judge, or you too will be judged. For in the same way you judge others, you will be judged, and with the measure you use, it will be measured to you."
>
> – Matthew 7:1, 2.

Here Jesus has all but promised us that if we laugh at a fool, we will come to discover that we ourselves have been the fools. In fact, the Proverbs seem to lump fools and mockers (or scorners) together as a single group (Proverbs 1:22).

More importantly, we must remember that our goal is to lead atheists to Christ – not to drive them farther away! Every time a scientist has said (correctly) that some particular fossil was millions of years old, and we laughed at him, judging him to be a fool, we have actually driven him farther from salvation. Now we have come to find that we ourselves have been the fools; we have been rude fools too – laughing openly at men who told us the truth. Consider this too, we have laughed at men who knew they spoke the truth and then watched us laugh.

Perhaps young-earth creationists have a zeal for God but, unfortunately, one which is not according to knowledge (Romans 10:2). Paul the Apostle originally channeled his powerful zeal for God against the early Church. What are we doing with ours? Young-earth creationists have, for the most part, merely generated smoke in an ill-fated attempt to conceal the true age of the universe. It would have been better if they had spent their time suggesting consistent structures of ideas which actually explain the scientific facts.

Far worse has been done than just making smoke! When erring young-earth arguments were made, how were they supported? Might more have been misrepresented than just the scientific facts? What about the scientists themselves? Consider this reaction by Harvard's Stephen Gould:

> "Faced with these facts of evolution and the philosophical bankruptcy of their own position, creationists rely upon distortion and innuendo to buttress their rhetorical claim. If I sound sharp or bitter, indeed I am – for I have become a major target of these practices."[1]

We have not used good science or good manners – it is well known that we have not. The evolutionists certainly have not

---

[1]Hen's Teeth and Horse's Toes, Stephen Jay Gould, C. 1983, W.W. Norton & Co., N.Y., p. 259.

been righteous either; but there will be time to address that – *after* we get our own act together.

Much of the teaching of evolution is founded upon "religious" atheism instead of scientific evidence. This is why evolutionists have religious faith in the "facts of evolution" where scientific caution would be more befitting a scientist. It would be nice if we creationists were in a position to point this out to them; but we are not likely to be heard. None of us will be taken seriously. It is assumed that all creationists are careless about their facts. If only we could just start afresh! But we cannot; sin always leaves scars – even when the real price has been paid for us.

We are losing an important battle – not against true science, but against another religion. Evolutionism is being preached in our schools and courtrooms and is beginning to interfere with our personal lives. We live in a society which willingly censors Biblical teaching of any kind from *our* public schools under the pretense of separation of church and state, yet *our* children are subjected to years of atheistic religious indoctrination. Furthermore, this mischief is funded by *our* tax dollars! There is a great deal at stake here; we desperately need to be taken seriously.

This is not likely to happen – especially since the books which young-earth creationists have been offering as a substitute contain fiction from cover to cover wherever the subject of dates occurs. If young-earth creationists had not done such a poor job of presenting God's creation, then we probably would not now be hearing atheists tell us that evolution is a "fact." The evolutionist's arguments only look good when they are compared to young-earth arguments; if the latter were not so bad, the former would not look at all plausible; the evolutionary view is not really convincing.

Evolutionism is not a position which men have been intellectually forced into by the world's data; God has left enough evidence. His own account of how He created our universe is pleading for recognition. Naturalistic evolution is a position which men have taken in spite of a great deal of data. Some have taken this position to avoid having to give an account to their Creator. Others might feel we creationists have left them no viable alternative.

There might still be hope, but we must stop insisting that the Bible tells a fairy tale about a ten-thousand year-old universe. Instead, we must reason out what the truth really is; then our preaching of Christianity could fit the universe's facts as well as the Bible's. Maybe then scientists would not try so hard to close their eyes and ears to the truth. As Paul says:

> "Since the creation of the world God's invisible qualities – his eternal power and divine nature – have been clearly seen, being understood from what has been made, so that *men are without excuse*."
>
> – Romans 1:20, Emphasis mine.

If we creationists would simply allow God's universe to speak for us instead of against us, then maybe a few more scientists would be able to see the hand of God at work in His creation and would come to know the saving truth.

> "God so loved the world that he gave his one and only Son, that whoever believes in him shall not perish but have eternal life. For God did not send his Son into the world to condemn the world, but to save the world through him."
>
> – Jesus, John 3:16, 17.

Appendices:

Wisdom's Call - Proverbs 8

Does not wisdom call out? Does not understanding raise her voice? On the heights along the way, where the paths meet, she takes her stand; beside the gates leading into the city, at the entrances, she cries aloud:

"To you, O men, I call out; I raise my voice to all mankind. You who are simple, gain prudence; you who are foolish, gain understanding. Listen, for I have worthy things to say; I open my lips to speak what is right. My mouth speaks what is true, for my lips detest wickedness. All the words of my mouth are just; none of them is crooked or perverse. To the discerning all of them are right; they are faultless to those who have knowledge. Choose my instruction instead of silver, knowledge rather than choice gold, for wisdom is more precious than rubies, and nothing you desire can compare with her.

"I, wisdom, dwell together with prudence; I possess knowledge and discretion. To fear the Lord is to hate evil; I hate pride and arrogance, evil behavior and perverse speech. Counsel and sound judgement are mine; I have understanding and power. By me kings reign and rulers make laws that are just; by me princes govern, and all nobles who rule on earth. I love those who love me, and those who seek me find me. With me are riches and honor, enduring wealth and prosperity. My fruit is better than fine gold; what I yield surpasses choice silver. I walk in the way of righteousness, along the paths of justice, bestowing wealth on those who love me and making their treasuries full.

"The Lord brought me forth as the first of his works, before his deeds of old; I was appointed from eternity, from the beginning, before the world began. When there were no oceans, I was given birth, when there were no springs abounding with water; before the mountains were settled in place, before the hills, I was given birth, before he made the earth or its fields or any of the dust of the world. I was there when he set the heavens in place, when he marked out the horizon on the face of the deep, when he established the clouds above and fixed securely the fountains of the deep, when he gave the sea its boundary so the waters would not overstep his command, and when he marked out the foundations of the earth. Then I was the craftsman at his side. I was filled with delight day after day, rejoicing always in his presence, rejoicing in his whole world and delighting in mankind.

"Now then, my sons, listen to me; blessed are those who keep my ways. Listen to my instruction and be wise; do not ignore it. Blessed is the man who listens to me, watching daily at my doors, waiting at my doorway. For whoever finds me finds life and receives favor from the Lord. But whoever fails to find me harms himself; all who hate me love death."

Appendix 1: Predictions

Here this author would like to make some predictions based on his understanding of how science and Genesis dovetail – the understanding which has been presented in this book. Those who are interested can test the claims made here with new scientific discoveries as they become available. This will provide a means to help determine if this author's understanding is correct or if we must look for another one.

1) Precambrian land plants (older than the oldest aquatic animals) should be discovered eventually.

2) No evidence will ever turn up that men preceding modern man ever wore clothes. (There was no knowledge of sin.) Although it can be argued that clothes were needed for warmth in the ice age climate (even if not for modesty) this author is betting (perhaps unnecessarily) that the Neanderthals and other pre-humans had sufficient body hair.

3) More evidence will continue to sharpen the separation between the Neanderthals and modern men. Archaic homo will eventually resolve into another distinct "kind." Evidence will eventually sharpen the difference between modern men and the Archaics as well.

4) Something will eventually turn up which will make sense out of the difference between the Ussher chronology (6 thousand years) and the carbon-14 chronology (about 40 thousand years).

5) Future young-earth "proofs" will continue to have errors in them.

Appendix 2: Arguments For 24-Hour Days

The following three quotations present arguments in support of the six-consecutive-24-hour-day position. These sources are quoted here in length to insure that the arguments are in context.

Source #1:

"Many Christians suggest that we should give God sufficient time to create this complex world by stretching the days of creation into hundreds of millions of years, so that each day of creation would equal an age. Is this legitimate? Well, actually it is amazing, when we begin to study the first chapter of Genesis, to discover that we have a built-in scheme of interpreting the length of these days, which shows that these must have been the same kind of days that we know today. For example, Genesis 1:14 says that God created the lights to divide the day from the night, and that they were to be for signs, for seasons, for days and years. If the days are ages, then what are years? If a day is an age, then what is a night? In other words, the whole passage becomes ridiculous when we begin to stretch or reinterpret the word 'day.'

"It is perfectly correct that in the Bible occasionally the word 'day' means a long, indefinite period of time, such as the 'Day of the Lord.' But never when the word 'day' is connected with a number does it mean anything other than a twenty-four hour period – for instance, the second day, the fourth day, the sixth day. Furthermore, whenever the word 'day' is connected with the qualifying phrase 'evening and morning,' we find a technical Hebrew expression that speaks of the rotation of the Earth's axis in reference to a fixed light source, passing through a night-day cycle.[1]

"Genesis chapter one is explained by Exodus 20:9, 11, when God spoke to Israel and said, 'Six days shalt thou labour, and do all thy work ... For in six days the Lord made heaven and earth, the sea, and all that in them is.' Obviously God was speaking in terms of literal days. No Jew in his right mind would think that God meant 'six indefinite periods shalt thou labor and rest a seventh indefinite period.'..."

– And God Created, Edited by Kelly L. Segraves, C. 1973, Creation-Science Research Center, San Diego, Ca. Volume II, pp. 62, 63. Bracketed footnote mine.

Source #2:

"As has been mentioned before, the Bible does not state the age of the world; consequently, several opinions are held by creationists. They can be divided easily into two major groupings: those who believe that the account of the creation of the world refers to six literal days, and those who feel that the six days were a figurative way of referring to indefinite periods of time. Both have some very good reasons for holding the positions they hold.

"Arguments for six literal days are:

"1. This would seem to be the normal way to interpret the passage (Gen. 1).

"2. The term 'day' when used elsewhere in Scripture usually means literal twenty-four hour days.

---

[1]Historically, the understanding that the earth turns on its axis was not even suggested until Aristarchus (born 310 BC) nor the theory made well known until Nicolaus Copernicus 1473-1543 AD. The Sleepwalkers, Arthur Koestler, C. 1959, The Universal Library, Grosset and Dunlap, N.Y., p. 49. It follows that this idea has no bearing whatsoever on the Biblical expression "evening and morning."

"3. It is hard to understand the reasoning of the argument of a Sabbath of rest on the seventh day after the six days of work creating the world if they were not six literal days (Gen. 2:2)."

– Creation Vs. Evolution Handbook, Thomas F. Heinze, C. 1973, Baker Book House, Grand Rapids, Michigan, pp. 104-105.

Source #3:

"... Many sincere and competent Biblical scholars have felt it so mandatory to accept the geological age system that they have prematurely settled on the so-called day-age theory as the recommended interpretation of Genesis 1. By this device, they seek more or less to equate the days of creation with the ages of evolutionary geology.

"However, this theory, no less than the gap theory, encounters numerous overwhelming objections which render it invalid. In the first place, the order of creative events narrated in Genesis 1 is very different from the accepted order of fossils in the rocks representing the geological ages. A number of these contradictions will be noted in the course of the exposition.

"Second, as already pointed out when discussing the gap theory, the geological ages are predicated on the fossil record, and fossils speak unequivocally of the reign of suffering and death in the world. The day-age theory, therefore, accepts as real the existence of death before sin, in direct contradiction to the Biblical teaching that death is a divine judgment on man's dominion because of man's sin (Romans 5:12). Thus it assumes that suffering and death comprise an integral part of God's work of creating and preparing the world for man; and this in effect pictures God as a sadistic ogre, not as the Biblical God of grace and love.

"Finally, the Biblical record itself makes it plain that the days of creation are literal days, not long indefinite ages. This will become conclusively evident as we examine the actual wording of these verses. Even though it may occasionally be possible for the Hebrew word for 'day' *(yom)* to mean an indefinite time, the specific context in Genesis 1 precludes any such meaning here.

"If the reader asks himself this question: 'Suppose the writer of Genesis wished to teach his readers that all things were created and made in six literal days, then what words would he use to best convey this thought?' he would have to answer that the writer would have used the actual words in Genesis 1. If he wished to convey the idea of long geological ages, however, he could surely have done it far more clearly and effectively in other words than in those which he selected. It was clearly his intent to teach creation in six literal days.

"Therefore, the only proper way to interpret Genesis 1 is not to 'interpret' it at all. That is, we accept the fact that it was meant to say exactly what it says. The 'days' are literal days and the events described happened in just the way described. This incomparable first chapter of Scripture tells us what we could never learn any other way – the history of creation. 'For in six days the Lord made heaven and earth, the sea, and all that in them is, and rested the seventh day: wherefore the Lord blessed the sabbath day, and hallowed it' (Exodus 20:11)."

– The Genesis Record, Henry M. Morris, C. 1976, Baker Book House, Grand Rapids, Michigan, pp. 53, 54.

Appendix 3: Real World Clocks

A Discussion for Those
Having a Technical Background

This appendix will try to explain the problem of synchronization of clocks in the same way in which it is often presented to beginning physics students. This illustration is silly enough to be interesting, while it is serious enough to accurately demonstrate the principles involved.

First we must picture in our minds a barn located anywhere in space (or on a planet) with two doors which open outwards on the two opposite front and back walls. We will assume that those two doors are 9 meters apart. Next we will picture a very fast traveling pole vaulter who is carrying a 10 meter pole. If the two doors are both open, the pole vaulter can run (carrying his pole) in through the front door, through the barn, and out through the back door without any difficulty. There will, of course, be a short period of time when his pole will extend out of the barn through both doors at the same time.

Next we will make our pole vaulter run very fast − 80% of the speed of light − and have him run through the barn again. This time the effects of Einstein's special theory of relativity will be apparent. If we stand next to the barn and observe the pole vaulter, his pole will appear to us (in our frame of reference) to have shortened to a new length equal to its original length (10 meters) times the square root of $(1-v^2/c^2)$. This is explained in detail on pp. 35, 36 of <u>Modern Physics: an Introductory</u>

Survey.[1] (The equation we are using is identified as "2-28" at the bottom of page 36.) Because our vaulter is running at 80% light speed, v/c, is 0.8 and so v^2/c^2 will become 0.64, which when subtracted from 1 leaves 0.36, whose square root is 0.6. When we multiply this factor by the original length of the pole (10 meters), we find that the pole now appears (to us at least) to be only 6 meters long.

So at this speed, the pole fits easily into the 9 meter barn. This means there is a very brief instant, while the vaulter is running through the barn, when we could very quickly slam both doors *at the same time* and open them again before there was any problem. We could, in principle at least, take a picture of the entire pole safely inside the barn with both doors closed. So far there is no problem.

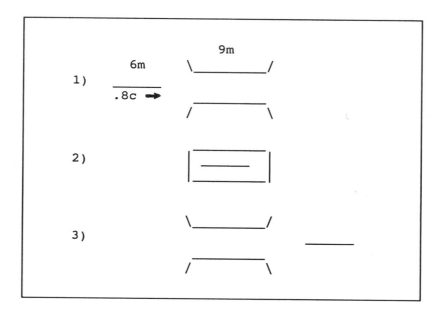

Now, how does this appear in the pole vaulter's frame of reference? It is a basic precept of relativity that all experiments

[1]*Modern Physics: an Introductory Survey*, Arthur Beiser, C. 1968, Addison-Wesley Publishing Co. Inc., Reading, Massachusetts, pp. 35, 36.

must give the same results when viewed from any frame of reference. Referring to <u>Modern Physics</u> again p. 29:

"As the Michelson-Morley experiment revealed, there is *no* ether,[2] and therefore no way of specifying any universal frame of reference. In other words, if we observe something changing its position with respect to us, we have no way (even in principle) of knowing whether *it* is moving or *we* are moving."

Emphasis theirs. Bracketed footnote mine.

So now we must look at this from the pole vaulter's frame of reference. Let us assume that it is the pole vaulter who is standing still (we ourselves will be standing beside him) and that it is the barn which is whizzing by around us at 80% light speed. This time it is the barn that appears to shorten by the same 0.6 factor (because the relative velocity, v/c, is still 0.8) – to a length of 9 meters times 0.6 which is equal to 5.4 meters. The 10 meter pole will no longer fit!

So what is going to happen when both of the barn's doors are closed *at the same time* as they were when we observed the way the universe behaves as seen from the barn's frame of reference? When the pole vaulter finally sits down after the experiment has been completed to discuss its results with the observer who stood by the barn, will they disagree as to whether or not there was a collision? Will the pole vaulter show his splintered pole as evidence and the barn observer show a motion picture sequence which proves that the pole was never even touched? Of course not! There cannot be any evidence, even in principle, which would prove in any absolute sense whether it was "they" or "we" who were moving.

As we saw in Chapter 4, the phrase *at the same time* is completely without meaning when high speeds or large distances are involved. If this phrase had any meaning, then we would have an unresolvable paradox here; but the phrase has no meaning and, as we will see, we do not have a paradox.

---

[2]The term "ether" refers to a hypothetical "fluid" that light waves were once thought to travel through. It was supposed to be the absolute universal stationary frame of reference.

Let us return to our example. We will have an observer, who is standing by the barn, decide when to close and re-open the two doors. (We will give him very long arms so that he can close and re-open both doors *at the same time*.)

What would happen, according to Einstein's laws, is that the pole vaulter would see this single event (both doors closing then re-opening) as two separate events. First he would see the barn's back door (the one he would pass through last) close and re-open while the leading end of his pole (although well inside the barn) was still a safe distance from that door. (2a). This would be before the hind end of the pole had made it into the barn at all.

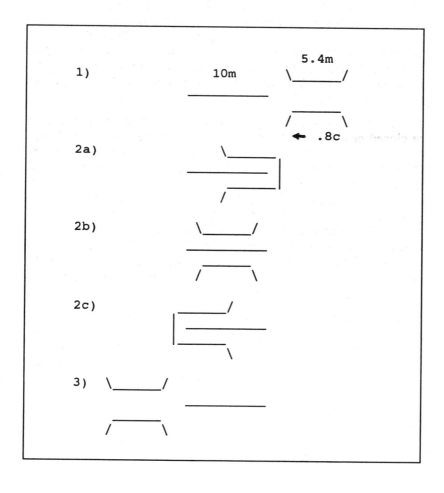

An instant later (*not at the same time*), he would see the front door (the one he has passed through first) close and re-open, but only after the hind end of the pole was safely inside the barn and clear of that door. (2c). At this time, the leading end of the pole would already be sticking through the other door and well out of the barn. The motion picture sequence which the pole vaulter might have filmed would confirm the absence of simultaneity as would any other recording instruments which he carried.

Only when we give up our pre-relativistic notion that two events can happen at exactly the same time – and that different observers will agree as to what this means – does the world really make sense. Otherwise there would be many paradoxes like the one just presented.

Finally, the conclusion of the preceding example will be confirmed with the best possible authorities – beginning with Nobel prize winner Richard P. Feynman, who before his recent death was a professor of theoretical physics at Caltech: "If we look at the situation carefully we see that events that occur at two separated places at the same time, as seen by Moe in S', do *not* happen at the same time as viewed by Joe in S."[3] (Emphasis his.) Next, another Nobel prize winner – Albert Einstein himself: "There is no absolute (independent of the space of reference) relation in space, and *no absolute relation in time between two events*,"[4] (Emphasis mine).

This is actually the way God made his universe! There really is no such thing as being at exactly the same time when two different events are separated by a distance.

---

[3]The Feynman Lectures on Physics, by Richard P. Feynman, C. 1963, Addison-Wesley Publishing Co., Reading, Mass. Vol. 1, p. 15-7.
[4]The Meaning of Relativity, by Albert Einstein, C. 1945, 1950, Princeton University Press, Princeton, pp. 30, 31.

Appendix 4: The Gap Theory

The gap theory places a huge time gap between the first and second verses of Genesis 1. According to this theory, Satan was evicted from heaven long ago and exiled to the earth. Satan then destroyed the earth between the first and second verses of Genesis 1 and God then re-created it in the rest of the chapter. This theory is an old attempt to correlate the supposedly short "days" of Genesis with the antiquity which science speaks of. It is presented in the notes of the Scofield Bible under Isaiah 45:18. Isaiah says:

"For this is what the Lord says – he who created the heavens, he is God; he who fashioned and made the earth, he founded it; he did not create it to be empty, but formed it to be inhabited ..."

–Isaiah 45:18.

Here the word "empty," and back in Genesis 1:2 the word "formless," are both translated from the Hebrew "tohuw." Genesis says that the earth was made "tohuw" (meaning empty, vain, waste, or something like "wild") but Isaiah says that it was not. Obviously one or the other of these verses needs a little bit of interpreting.

What the Scofield Bible did with this pair in its notes was to translate the word "was" in Genesis 1:2 as "became." This is acceptable as far as the Hebrew is concerned. Thus Genesis 1:2 would read, "And the earth *became* without form and void ..."

So even though God did not *originally* create the earth "tohuw" it later *became* "tohuw" as a result of Satan's fall.

There is a much simpler way to interpret Isaiah. Notice that God "did not create the earth empty (tohuw), *but* formed it to be inhabited." What Isaiah means here is easily seen from the implied comparison between the two states of the earth; what is meant by "tohuw" here is "uninhabited" − or in this particular context "not to be inhabited." Isaiah is contrasting the earth's initial state with the fact that it was later to be inhabited. Whatever else a person believes, they must accept the fact that the world was uninhabited at the time when God first created it. All that Isaiah 45:18 says is that it was not intended that it should remain that way forever.[1]

This is really a much cleaner way to interpret the Bible. There is no need to hypothesize a giant gap between the first two verses of Genesis − one which God has said nothing about and for which there is no scientific evidence. We do not need to claim that Satan came along and messed the world up. The Bible tells us that Adam did that.

Examination of those verses where Satan's fall is referred to (Isaiah 14:1-20, Ezekiel 28:11-19, Luke 10:18, Revelation 12:3-13) does not unambiguously identify the event as being past or future. Good arguments can be made either way. For example, in Luke 10:18 Jesus says, "I saw Satan fall like lightning from heaven." This would seem to refer to a past event; but then Jesus might have been speaking prophetically. The Bible also seems to tell us that Satan had not yet been evicted from heaven even as recently as Job's time. Job 1:6 says, "One day the angels came to present themselves before the Lord, and Satan also came with them." This verse establishes that Satan had access to heaven at that time. Satan is regarded as the accuser of the brethren before God even today (Rev. 12:10). From this it would seem that he has access to heaven and has not yet, even at this present time, been evicted.

---

[1]The same conclusion will be reached by studying Jeremiah 4:23-28. The phrase "formless and empty" is elaborated upon in this passage emphasizing the absence of inhabitation, e.g. light gone, no people, birds flown away, towns in ruins.

To avoid this sequencing difficulty, Christians sometimes divide the casting down of Satan into two separate parts: first the casting down to earth and later the final casting out of heaven. This is cumbersome at best; but as was explained back in Chapter 4, there is another explanation. The very nature of time is not as simple as we normally presume.

Consider what we really mean when we say, "at this present time" – "now" as it appears to us in our earthly frame of reference or "now" as it appears to God in His? According to Einstein's laws, it can be impossible to know, even in principle, which of two widely separated events came first and which second – and here we are dealing with one event in heaven and another on earth! Satan is being cast from heaven to earth. Here the problem becomes vastly more difficult.

God is the one who calls things which are not as though they were (Romans 4:17) and knows what is going to happen in our future. The relationship of time between heaven, where He resides, and earth seems to be past our understanding. This is true even if the relationship of time between two observers in different earthly frames of reference isn't already completely past our understanding. But perhaps we have grasped just enough of a taste of the truth from studying time in God's creation to give us a glimmer of what sort of thing the heavenly reality might be. It will *not* be a simple question of "before" or "after" as we understand those terms.

In any case, no matter how one chooses to treat the fall of Satan, there is no reason, scientific or scriptural to hypothesize a time gap between the first two verses of Genesis 1. The scientific account of the universe's creation matches Genesis without any supposed time gap. The Bible says nothing about Satan ever having destroyed the world. We should not assume any such theory when we have not been provided with either scientific or scriptural reason to do so.

Appendix 5: The Ussher Chronology

This appendix will attempt to reconstruct Archbishop James Ussher's 1650 AD calculation of the year in which God created Adam. Ussher used the genealogies provided in the Bible to reach a date of 4004 BC. (As explained in Chapter 6, this does not agree well at all with the scientific evidence which would place the first actual men *many* thousands of years earlier.)

King Solomon will serve as a starting point from which to work backward. Solomon was a modern enough figure that he can be tied to history fairly well – at least rough dates are available. Solomon assumed the throne of Israel at about 960 BC.[1] This date is probably fairly accurate; but in any case it will certainly be accurate enough for the present purpose; after all, this concerns an error of about thirty thousand years.

The chronology can be extended backward from Solomon to Adam one step at a time as follows: 1 Kings 6:1 tells us that 480 years elapsed between the time the children of Israel came out of the land of Egypt and the fourth year of Solomon's reign. This means that 476 of those years had elapsed by the year in which Solomon assumed the throne (960 BC). So it may be concluded that the children of Israel left Egypt 476 years before 960 BC, or in about the year 1436 BC.

Next Exodus 12:40 tells us that the children of Israel stayed in Egypt for 430 years before Moses led them out.[2] From this it

---

[1]The Conquest of Civilization, James Henry Breasted, C. 1926, 1938, The Literary Guild of America, Inc., N.Y., p. 187. (This event was synchronous with the death of King David.)

[2]See also Acts 13:17-20.

can be calculated that the children of Israel entered Egypt about 1866 BC. This period may include the period preceding the captivity because a shorter span of time is given in Acts 7:6 for the captivity itself. Presumably this 430 year period in Egypt began when Jacob moved there. This should be at least reasonably close to the actual beginning of that period. (But this is an assumption.) As we learn from Genesis 47:28, Jacob had lived in Egypt for seventeen years at the time of his death at the age of 147 years. It follows that Jacob's age was 130 years when he moved into Egypt. This means that Jacob was born 130 years before 1866 BC or somewhere near the year 1996 BC.

Next, Genesis 25:26 informs us that Jacob's father Isaac was sixty years old when Jacob was born. This puts the birth of Isaac at about 2056 BC. Similarly, from Genesis 21:5 we find that Abraham was a hundred years old when Isaac was born, putting the birth of Abraham at about 2156 BC.

From this point back to Adam the dates come quite rapidly. Chapters 5 and 11 of Genesis are summarized here:

Genesis 11:10-26:

Terah born 70 years before Abraham .... 2226 BC[3]
Nahor born 29 years before Terah .... 2255 BC
Serug born 30 years before Nahor .... 2285 BC
Reu born 32 years before Serug .... 2317 BC
Peleg born 30 years before Reu .... 2347 BC
Eber born 34 years before Peleg .... 2381 BC
Salah born 30 years before Eber .... 2411 BC
Arphaxad born 35 years before Salah .... 2446 BC
Shem born 100 years before Arphaxad .... 2546 BC

---

[3] Actually Genesis 11:26 says, "After Terah had lived 70 years, he became the father of Abram, Nahor and Haran." The three were probably each born in different years. Although Abram is listed first (being the most important from the Jewish perspective), it appears from other scripture that he was not actually the first born of the three. Genesis 11:32 tells us that Terah died in Haran at the age of 205. We see from Acts 7:4 that Abram (Abraham) moved from Haran to Israel only after Terah died. And finally Genesis 12:4 tells us that Abram was 75 when he left Haran. This means that Terah must have been

---

Genesis 5:3-32:

Noah was born 500 years before Shem .... 3046 BC[4]
Lamech was born 182 years before Noah .... 3228 BC
Methuselah was born 187 years before Lamech ..... 3415 BC
Enoch was born 65 years before Methuselah .... 3480 BC
Jared was born 162 years before Enoch .... 3642 BC
Mahalaleel was born 65 years before Jared .... 3707 BC
Cainan was born 70 years before Mahalaleel .... 3777 BC
Enos was born 90 years before Cainan .... 3867 BC
Seth was born 105 years before Enos .... 3972 BC
Adam was made 130 years before Seth was born .... 4102 BC

Ussher probably used some different verses than these and probably tied them to a different point in history as well. Still, 4102 BC. agrees well enough with his 4004 BC. This is where the 6000-year-old figure for the age of the earth comes from; 4000 years BC. plus nearly 2000 years AD. adds up to about 6000 years ago. Actually this calculation does not give the date of the earth's creation – only of Adam's, which was sometime during the sixth "day" – and, of course, the Bible does not say how long the "days" of Genesis really were. Still, this chronology provides enough trouble even if it only applies to Adam!

It is normally assumed that there are many gaps in the Biblical genealogies; most creationists agree there are thousands

---

about 130 (or older) when Abram was born. This introduces a 60 year (or greater) error to the traditional chronology.

[4]Here, in Genesis 5:32 the text says, "After Noah was 500 years old, he became the father of Shem, Ham and Japheth." It is improbable that all three were born within the same year. There are clues as to exactly when Shem was born. Genesis 11:10 says that when Shem begat Arphaxad he was 100 years old and that Arphaxad was born two years after the flood. This means that Shem was 98 when the flood ended. Genesis 8:13 tells us that the flood ended when Noah was 601. Noah would have to have been about 503 when Shem was born if he were to be 601 years old when Shem was 98. This only introduces a three-year error.

of years' worth. The only remaining dispute is over just how many thousands there may be.

Bibliography

Aardsma, Gerald E., "Has the Speed of Light Decayed?" Institute for Creation Research, I.C.R. Technical Report #1187.

Ackerman, Paul D., It's a Young World After All, Exciting Evidences for Recent Creation, C. 1986, Baker Book House, Grand Rapids, Michigan 49506.

Barendsen, G.W., "Yale Natural Radiocarbon Measurements," SCIENCE, November 1, 1957, Vol. 126, No. 3279, p. 911.

Barnes, Thomas G., Origin and Destiny of the Earth's Magnetic Field, 1973, Institute for Creation Research, San Diego, Ca.

Beiser, Arthur, Modern Physics: an Introductory Survey, C. 1968, Addison-Wesley Publishing Co. Inc. Reading, Massachusetts.

Benditt, John, "Grave Doubts, The Neanderthals may not have buried their dead after all," SCIENTIFIC AMERICAN, June 1989, Vol. 260, No. 6, pp. 32, 33.

Boardman, William W. Jr. et al, Science and Creation, C. 1973, Creation-Science Research Center, San Diego, Ca.

Bok, Bart J., "The Milky Way Galaxy," SCIENTIFIC AMERICAN, March 1981, Vol. 244, No. 3, pp. 92+.

Breasted, James Henry, Conquest of Civilization, C. 1926, 1938, The Literary Guild of America, Inc., N.Y.

Calder, Nigel, Einstein's Universe, C. 1979, The Viking Press, N.Y.

Chapman, Clark R., "Encounter! Voyager 2 Explores the Uranian System," THE PLANETARY REPORT, March/April 1986, Vol. VI, No. 2, pp. 8-12.

Chronic, Halka, <u>Pages of Stone</u>, C. 1984, The Mountaineers, 306 2nd Avenue West, Seattle, Washington 98119.

Cloud, Preston, <u>Oasis in Space, Earth History from the Beginning</u>, C. 1988, W.W. Norton and Company, N.Y.

Einstein, Albert, <u>The Meaning of Relativity</u>, C. 1945, Princeton University Press, Princeton.

Einstein, Albert, <u>Relativity</u>, C. 1931, Crown Publishers, N.Y.

Feynman, Richard P., <u>The Feynman Lectures on Physics</u>, C. 1963, Addison-Wesley Publishing Co., Reading, Massachusetts, Vol. 1.

<u>Gesenius' Hebrew-Chaldee Lexicon to the Old Testament</u>, C. 1979, Baker Book House Co., Grand Rapids, Michigan.

Gish, Duane T., <u>Evolution: The Fossils Say No!</u>, C. 1979, Creation-Life Publishers. San Diego, Ca.

Gould, Stephen Jay, <u>Hen's Teeth and Horse's Toes</u>, C. 1983, W.W. Norton and Company N.Y.

Gould, Stephen Jay, <u>The Panda's Thumb</u>, C. 1980, W.W. Norton and Co.

Gowlett, John, <u>Ascent to Civilization</u>, C. 1984, Alfred A. Knopf Inc., N.Y.

Gregory, Stephen A. and Laird A. Thompson, "Superclusters and Voids in the Distribution of Galaxies," SCIENTIFIC AMERICAN, March 1982, Vol. 246, No. 3, p. 106.

Gribbin, John, <u>Our Changing Planet</u>, C. 1977, Thomas Y. Crowell Company, N.Y.

Hafele, J.C. and Richard E. Keating, "Around the World Atomic Clocks: Observed Relativistic Time Gains," SCIENCE, July 14, 1972, Vol. 177, No. 4044, pp. 168-170.

Hafele, J.C. and Richard E. Keating, "Around the World Atomic Clocks: Predicted Relativistic Time Gains," SCIENCE, July 14, 1972, Vol. 177, No. 4044, pp. 166-168.

Hawkes, Jacquetta, <u>Atlas of Ancient Archaeology</u>, C. 1974, McGraw-Hill Book Company, N.Y.

Heinze, Thomas F., <u>Creation Vs. Evolution Handbook</u>, C. 1973, Baker Book House, Grand Rapids, Michigan.

Henbest, Nigel, <u>Mysteries of the Universe</u>, C. 1981, Van Nostrand Reinhold Company, N.Y.

Hensley, W.K., et al, "Pressure Dependence of the Radioactive Decay Constant of Beryllium-7," SCIENCE, September 21, 1973, Vol. 181, No. 4105, pp. 1164, 1165.

Hitch, Charles J., "Dendrochronology and Serendipity," AMERICAN SCIENTIST, May-June 1982, Vol. 70, No. 3, pp. 300+.

Hodge, Paul W., "The Andromeda Galaxy," SCIENTIFIC AMERICAN, January 1981, Vol. 244, No. 1, pp. 92-101.

Horne, R.A., Marine Chemistry, C. 1979, Wiley-Interscience, N.Y.

Hoyle, Fred and Chandra Wickramasinghe, Evolution From Space, C. 1981, Simon and Schuster Inc., N.Y.

Hummel, Charles E., The Galileo Connection, C. 1986, Inter Varsity Press, Downers Grove, Illinois, 60515.

Jastrow, Robert, God and the Astronomers, C. 1978, W.W. Norton and Company, Inc., N.Y.

Johanson, Donald and Maitland Edey, Lucy: the Beginnings of Humankind, C. 1981, Warner Books, N.Y.

Keith, M.L. and G.M. Anderson, "Radiocarbon Dating: Fictitious Results with Mollusk Shells," SCIENCE, August 16, 1963, Vol. 141, No. 3581, pp. 634+.

Keller, Phillip, A Shepherd Looks at Psalm 23, C. 1970, Zondervan, Grand Rapids, Michigan.

Koestler, Arthur, The Sleepwalkers, C. 1959, The Universal Library, Grosset and Dunlap, N.Y.

Leakey, Richard E., The Making of Mankind, C. 1981, E.P. Dutton, N.Y.

Lewin, Roger, Human Evolution: an Illustrated Introduction, C. 1984, W.H. Freeman and Company, N.Y.

Lunan, Duncan, New Worlds For Old, C. 1979, William Morrow and Company, Inc., N.Y.

McDowell, Josh, Reasons Skeptics Should Consider Christianity, C. 1981, Here's Life Publishers. P.O. Box 1576, San Bernardino, CA 92402.

McKenzie, A.E.E., A Second Course of Light, 1956 - reprinted 1965, Cambridge University Press, Great Britain.

McMenamin, Mark A.S., "The Emergence of Animals," SCIENTIFIC AMERICAN, April 1987, Vol. 256, No. 4, pp. 94+.

Miller, Russell, <u>Continents in Collision</u>, C. 1983, Time-Life Books, Alexandria, Virginia.

Milne, Lorus and Margery, <u>The Audubon Society Field Guide to North American Insects and Spiders</u>, C. 1980, Alfred A. Knopf Inc., N.Y.

Morris, Henry M., <u>The Genesis Record</u>, C. 1976, Baker Book House, Grand Rapids, Michigan.

Morris, Henry M., <u>Scientific Creationism</u>, C. 1974, Master Books, El Cajon, Ca.

Nobel, C.S. and J.J. Naughton, "Deep-Ocean Basalts: Inert Gas Content and Uncertainties in Age Dating," SCIENCE, October 11, 1968, Vol. 162, No. 3850, pp. 265+.

Norman, Trevor and Barry Setterfield, <u>The Atomic Constants, Light, and Time</u>," C. 1987, Stanford Research Institute International, 333 Ravenswood Ave. Menlo Park, California, 94025.

Osmer, Patrick S., "Quasars as Probes of the Distant and Early Universe," SCIENTIFIC AMERICAN, February 1982, Vol. 246, No. 2, p. 126.

Parkinson, John H., Leslie V. Morrison and F. Richard Stephenson, "The Consistency of the Solar Diameter Over the Past 250 Years," NATURE, December 11, 1980, Vol. 288, pp. 548-549.

Renfrew, Colin, "Carbon 14 and the Prehistory of Europe," SCIENTIFIC AMERICAN, October 1971, Vol. 225, No. 4, pp. 63-72.

Ross, Philip E., "Hard Words," SCIENTIFIC AMERICAN, April 1991, Vol. 264, No. 4, pp. 138-147.

Setterfield, Barry, <u>Geological Time and Scriptural Chronology</u>, Available from: Barry Setterfield, Box 318, Blackwood, S.A., 5051 Australia.

Schramm, David N. and Gary Steigman, "Particle Accelerators Test Cosmological Theory," SCIENTIFIC AMERICAN, June 1988, Vol. 258, No. 6, pp. 66+.

Schwarcz, H.P., et al, "ESR dates for the hominid burial site of Qafzeh in Israel," JOURNAL OF HUMAN EVOLUTION, December 1988, Vol. 17, No. 8, pp. 733-737.

Sears, Francis Weston, <u>Mechanics, Heat, and Sound</u>, C. 1950, Addison-Wesley Publishing Company, Inc. Reading, Massachusetts.

Segraves, Kelly L., And God Created, (Vol. 2) C. 1973, Creation-Science Research Center, San Diego, Ca.

Shannon, Foster H., God is Light, C. 1981, Green Leaf Press, P.O. Box 5, Campbell, Ca. 95008.

Shapiro, Robert, Origins: a Skeptic's Guide to the Creation of Life on Earth, C. 1986, Summit Books, N.Y.

Smith, David G., The Cambridge Encyclopedia of Earth Sciences, C. 1981, Crown Publishers Inc. / Cambridge University Press, N.Y.

Spenser, Edmund, The Faerie Queen, J.M. Dent and Sons Ltd., London, and E.P. Dutton & Co. Inc., N.Y., 1910 edition.

Strong, James, Strong's Exhaustive Concordance of the Bible, Riverside Book and Bible House, Iowa Falls, Iowa 50126.

Tarling, D.H., Palaeomagnetism, Principles and Applications in Geology, Geophysics and Archaeology, C. 1983, Chapman and Hall, London.

Thompson, Ida, The Audubon Society Field Guide to North American Fossils, Alfred A. Knopf, N.Y.

Turner, Grenville, "Argon-40/Argon-39 Dating of Lunar Rock Samples," SCIENCE, January 30, 1970, Vol. 167, No. 3918, pp. 466+.

Waechter, John, Prehistoric Man: the Fascinating Story of Man's Evolution, C. 1977, Octopus Books Limited, London.

Weast, Robert C., Handbook of Chemistry and Physics 49th Edition, Ph.D., C. 1964, The Chemical Rubber Company, 18901 Cranwood Parkway, Cleveland, Ohio, 44128.

Weinberg, Steven, The First Three Minutes, A Modern View of the Origin of the Universe, Updated Edition, C. 1977, 1988, Basic Books, Inc., Publishers, N.Y.

White, Randall, "Visual Thinking in the Ice Age," SCIENTIFIC AMERICAN, July 1989, Vol. 261, No. 1, p. 92.

Wiseman, P.J., Ancient Records and the Structure of Genesis, C. 1985, Thomas Nelson Publishers, Nashville.

Woosley, Stan and Tom Weaver, "The Great Supernova of 1987," SCIENTIFIC AMERICAN, August 1989, Vol. 261, No. 2, p. 32.

Young, Robert, Young's Concordance to the Bible, C. 1964, William B. Eerdmans Publishing Company, Grand Rapids, Michigan.

Youngblood, Ronald, The Genesis Debate, C. 1986, Thomas Nelson Publishers, Nashville.

Apollo 16, Preliminary Report, 1972, NASA SP-315.

"At the Moon Conference: Consensus and Conflict," SCIENCE NEWS, January 23, 1971, Vol. 99, No. 4, p. 62.

"Lunar Sciences: Luna 16, An Unusual Core," SCIENCE NEWS, January 23, 1971, Vol. 99, No. 4, p. 65.

The Soviet-American Conference on Cosmochemistry of the Moon and Planets, 1977, NASA SP-370, Vol. 2.

"Velocity of Light 300 Years Ago," SKY & TELESCOPE, June 1973, Vol. 45, No. 6, pp. 353-354.

Bibles:

The Holy Bible, New International Version, C. 1973, 1978, 1984, Zondervan Bible Publishers, Grand Rapids, Michigan.

The Interlinear Bible, Jay P. Green Sr., C. 1976, Baker Book House, Grand Rapids Michigan.

The Interlinear Greek-English New Testament, Rev. Alfred Marshall D. Litt., C. 1958, Zondervan Publishing House, Grand Rapids, Michigan.

The Living Bible, C. 1971, Tyndale House Publishers, Wheaton, Illinois 60187.

The New American Standard Bible, C. 1960, Foundation Press Publications, La Habra, California.

The New Scofield Reference Edition, Holy Bible, Authorized King James Version, Ed. C.I. Scofield, D.D., C. 1967, Oxford University Press, N.Y.

The NIV Interlinear Hebrew-English Old Testament, Vol. 1, Ed. John R. Kohlenberger, C. 1979, Zondervan Publishing house, Grand Rapids, Michigan.

Scriptural Index

Topical Index

Matter 105-111 143
  Hebrew for 108 109 111
Metaphor 68 104
Meteor 115
Meteoritic dust 79-85 100
Michelson/Morley experiment
  24 64-65 162
Michelson, A.A. 63-65
Micrometeorites 82
Millennium 9 11 48
Miocene 97
Miracles 48 104
Mistakes 9 18 22 27-31 52 61
  76 98 101 117 (see also
  errors)
Mockers 17-18 150
Mollusks, carbon-14 dating of
  92
Monroe, M. 107
Moon 15 24 54 56 127 128
  130 131 146
  dust 79-85
Morning, Hebrew for 41-43
  (see also evening and
  morning)
Morris, H. 75 81 86 99-101
  122 140 159
Moses 12 47 49 168
Motion, relative 160-164
Mountains 118
Moved, Hebrew for 111-112
Mutations 26
NASA 80 82 84-85
Natural selection 26
Nature of God 16 22 51 53 54
  67-68 71 88 152
Neanderthal man 135-138 140
  155
Nebular dust 111-116 143 144
Neutrons 89 90

New American Standard Bible
  33 43 44
New Testament 28 37 41 46
Nitrogen 89-91 116 120
Noah 170
Noah's flood 129 170
Nobel prize 63 164
Noble birth 35
Norman, T. 58-62 66
Nuclear fusion 113
Nucleosynthesis 107
Monroe, M. 107
Number plus day 43-45
Observer-true 30-31 128
Obstacles 52
Ocean of storms, Lunar 80 81
Oceans 86 87 95 99 118-120
  144-145
Old Testament 13 28
Old-earth 16 34 50 70 72 120
  133
Original sin 13 49
Overlapping days 121 122
  147
Ox 48
Oxygen 91 125 145
Ozone 125
Paleomagnetism 98 99
Pangea 119
Parables 34 36 71
Parallax, stellar 31
Penzias 107
Pettersson, H. 79-82
Photon 67
Photosynthesis 26 127
Physical death 11-14 41 50
Physics 26 63 65 106 160
Piltdown man 70
Plain reading 15-16 33
Planets 54 108-113
Plants 48-49 91 118 **121-127**
  132 145 155

About The Author

Don Stoner was introduced to the controversy surrounding Genesis in the second grade when he came home from school and asked his father why he was taught in Sunday school that the earth was created in six days and in elementary school that it was created over a much greater period of time. Fortunately, answers were available; his grandfather, Peter W. Stoner, was the author of Science Speaks, a best seller on the subject of scientific proof of the inerrancy of prophecy and the Bible. The subject has fascinated Don since and over the years he has himself become an authority on the subject of creation.

Don went on to receive his BS in Physics and has been awarded two U.S. patents. Two of the more notable projects he has been involved with professionally include the development of the optical disc and the Precision Motion Chiptester. Don has a wife Debbie, four daughters and one son.